THE GRIEVING HEART

A SIMPLE GUIDE
TO HEALING FROM LIFE'S
MANY LOSSES

written and edited by

Bob Dorsett, Ed.D.

"The Grieving Heart: a simple guide to healing from life's many losses"

First Printing: Copyright © 2011 by Bob Dorsett, LLC
Second Printing: Copyright © 2014 by Bob Dorsett, LLC

Published 2011 and 2014 by Bob Dorsett, LLC.

ISBN: 978-0-9704946-1-0

1. Grief   2. Loss (psychological aspects)   3. Bereavement   4. Death (psychological aspects)
5. Self help   6.Teenagers-death   7. Child-death   8. Spouse-death

---

**PURCHASING "THE GRIEVING HEART" FOR PERSONAL
or GRIEF SUPPORT AGENCIES' USE**

Additional copies may be ordered on Amazon.com, or by ordering directly from Bob Dorsett for $14.00 (free shipping included within the continuous United States): for mailing instructions *www.silentseas.net (website)* or *griefsupport@silentseas*.net

If grief support agencies wish to purchase these articles in a printable format in order to give them to their clients, the cost for a CD of the articles in printable format is $250. For further information, please email Bob Dorsett: *griefsupport@silentseas.net*. These agencies may print personal contact information at the bottom of each article. Authorship on each article should be acknowledged as follows: "This article was published in 'The Grieving Heart: a simple guide to healing from life's many losses' by Bob Dorsett,LLC (*www.silentseas.net*)" These purchased articles may not be given to other organizations.

Bob Dorsett's website is: *www.silentseas.net*

Printed in USA by 48HrBooks (*www.48HrBooks.com*)

ACKNOWLEDGMENTS

I acknowledge Chris Angell, co-writer of these articles, whose professional commitment to quality, insight and compassion is evident throughout this book.

I thank Marylee Bytheriver, Executive Director, Hospice of Humboldt, Eureka, California for supporting this writing project as a contribution to the bereavement program.

I also acknowledge Linda Kamenetzky, former Director of Social Services, Hospice of Humboldt, for her vision to create this writing project.

"Healing Hands" photograph on the front cover of this book was contributed by
Arthur Rosch, www.artrosch.com

DEDICATION

This book is dedicated to all grieving beings,

and to those who accompany them

on their healing journey.

Why a simple book on healing from your losses?

"The Grieving Heart" is an easy-to-follow guide that can help you heal from the many possible deaths that you may experience in your lifetime. In addition, it offers suggestions on how to support others who have experienced these losses.

 **Most of us do not like to think about death, or the grief that follows**. To avoid the thought of becoming older, some people color their hair, use wrinkle-hiding creams, have facelifts or other interventions to try to postpone aging, and the thought of dying. Also, our culture encourages us to ignore the grief that naturally follows from the deaths of our loved ones by actions such as keeping busy, drinking alcohol, or suppressing feelings. In spite of these efforts, death and grief occur, and the longer we live, the more we will experience the death of family, friends and pets. The natural and inevitable result of these losses is grief.

Why heal your grief? A common perception is that grief will resolve itself if you ignore it. However, ignoring grief is a temporary and dangerous fix. Grief does not go away without personal effort. It may appear to go away, but grief can settle into your psyche and your body with serious consequences. It can diminish your ability to be truly intimate, affect your sleeping, or harm your health. Unhealed grief can result in expressing inappropriate anger, driving recklessly, or making mountains out of molehills. Unresolved grief limits your ability to live fully, love completely, and live in the present moment.

Why a simple guide for healing grief? If you are open to facing and healing your grief, you may be among the many people who feel that they don't have the energy or the interest to read an entire book offering suggestions on healing from grief. For this reason, I and a colleague wrote and edited for hospice these easy-to-read and easy-to-apply articles on healing from grief. They are a summary of some of the best bereavement literature available, and each article is only one or two pages in length. Also this book will help guide you through different losses because the path to healing from the many diverse types of deaths can vary widely. For example, healing from an expected death is distinctly different from recovering from a sudden death due to a car accident, or a suicide. The paths toward healing from the death of a child, a parent, a sibling, or a spouse can be notably different. Below are topics covered in this book:

---

*understanding grief   *myths about grief   *rituals that heal   *tools that help heal grief   *helping the dying
*grief before the loss *grief websites *partner/spouse death *widow/widower support *pet death *parent death
*sudden/traumatic death *sister/brother death *adult child death * healing from many losses felt in a brief time
*child death *helping your grieving teen *talking to your child about death *internet grief help *death by suicide
*getting through the first anniversary, the holidays and those special days   *grieving person's bill of rights
*how to support someone who is grieving (even if you are grieving)   * how men heal from their grief

---

These articles can serve as guides in your healing process, but keep in mind that healing from grief requires active participation on your part. Reading the articles is only the first step. If you do the suggested work, you will heal from your loss. Your body and heart naturally want to heal, and you need to travel the path consciously in order for healing to take place.

If you do wish to read further on any particular bereavement topic, many of these articles present background material and books that you can access through your local bookstore or the Internet. In addition to following the suggestions offered in these articles, it may be beneficial to participate in a grief support group provided free of charge by your local hospice, or in private grief counseling if this suits you better. There are also many cities where grief support groups for children and teens are available.

Bob Dorsett

Table of Contents

GENERAL GRIEF INFORMATION

GRIEF SUPPORT FOR SPECIAL OCCASIONS

27. **"getting through the first anniversary of your loved one's death"** - With the first anniversary of your loved one's death on the horizon, it may be helpful for you to keep in mind that your grief may return with intensity. There are no hard and fast rules for grieving, yet it may be helpful to be prepared for what is referred to as "anniversary grief."

29. **"how will I get through the holidays?"** - You may approach the holidays with sadness as you remember loved ones you have lost. There may be a sense of dread about upcoming events and social gatherings. Perhaps you feel pressure to participate when you would rather not. You may hope for opportunities to share special memories but fear bringing them up in order to protect others from feeling the pain of loss. This article will offer suggestions on how to get through the holidays.

31. **"it won't be the same this year... getting through those special days"** - When someone we love dies, we especially miss them on those special days. You may approach these days with dread. While friends and family gather, you may feel lonely and sad. This article will give you helpful suggestions on dealing with those special days.

MEN HEALING FROM THEIR GRIEF

33. **"a hero's journey... how men heal from their grief"** - Much has been written about men's lack of emotional expressiveness because they tend to grieve in a private and quiet manner. Many people believe that the healing of grief is only accomplished through crying and talking. However, there are other ways. It's more useful to focus on the strengths men naturally possess.

HELPING SOMEONE WHO IS DYING

35. **"helping your loved one who is dying"** - Your friend or family member, someone you care deeply for, is dying. This is an extremely difficult time for you, your loved one, and all who care about her or him. You may be asking yourself, "How can I be of best help and comfort?" This article will offer simple suggestions on helping your dying loved one and yourself.

TEENS AND GRIEF

37. **"helping your teen cope with grief"** - Each year thousands of teenagers experience the death of someone they love. When a parent, sibling, friend or relative dies, teens may feel the overwhelming loss of someone who helped shape their developing self-identities, yet they may not know how to express their grief in healthy ways. This article will offer suggestions on how to help your teen.

39. **"teens help other teens on the Internet with death and grieving"** - Helpful websites for teens to communicate with other teens on the Internet regarding their grief.

CHILDREN AND DEATH

40. **"talking to your child about death"** - There has been a death in your family, and you see sadness in your child. When you see your child grieve like this, you wonder how you can best comfort and support her or him. This article may give you some guidance and suggestions on how to help.

42. **"healing when your child dies...a lifetime journey"** - The death of a child is one of the most difficult deaths to heal from. This article offers understanding and insight into this healing process for parents, siblings, and grandparents, as well as helpful reference materials.

GRIEF SUPPORT ON THE INTERNET

44. **"websites that will help you heal and find support"** - For those who are comfortable with communicating on the Internet, this article offers a number of websites where you can communicate with others on a variety of grief topics.

SUPPORTING A GRIEVING PERSON

45. **"how to support someone who is grieving (...even if you are grieving)"** - Lack of information on how to support someone who is grieving is common in our culture. This article will give you simple to understand guidelines on what to say and what not to say to a grieving person.

when you are grieving

Someone whom you love has died, or is dying, and you feel sadness. You may be asking, "Why do I hurt so much?" If you can take a moment, I would like to talk with you about the hurt and sadness that you are experiencing.

Everybody at one time or another feels grief because of the death of a loved one. This deep hurt is only possible when someone we are close to dies. We rely on each other. We spend many years dependent on our parents, other adults and children. We have families. We make friends. We have neighbors.

It is a part of our makeup to form lasting bonds of caring and affection with other people. We fall in love and long for the love of another person. If we lived our lives separately from other people, and did not need to rely on others, the loss or death of another would have little impact.

Because we form deep attachments, we are vulnerable.

Because we depend on other people, because they matter to us, they become a part of us and cannot be replaced. When someone is gone from our lives, someone with whom we have a heart attachment, a piece of us has been torn away. The loss wounds us deeply. This wound is called "grief."

The grief wound can be healed, but it will take time.

Grieving is the way we heal from this wound. Through the process of mourning, the outward expression of inner grief, we gradually accept the loss and heal. At the end of mourning, there is still a feeling of sadness, but it is not the deep hurt we have felt before. With the sadness, we still have happy memories of our loved one who has died.

There are no hard and fast rules for how people grieve.

Grief may be more intense and more prolonged the more you relied on, or were bonded to, the person or pet that died. Also some deaths tend to be more difficult: the loss of a child, death from a suicide, or an unexpected death, to name a few.

I would like to share with you what happens to our bodies, to our hearts, and to our lives when we experience grief. Before I talk about these changes, I want you to know that they are absolutely normal. There is nothing wrong with anyone who experiences these reactions. However, each person's response to grief is unique. Therefore you may or may not experience some or all of these changes.

There are physical changes such as:

- ❖ You may feel tired more easily.
- ❖ You may experience loss of energy and even numbness.
- ❖ You may not sleep well.
- ❖ You may sleep a lot.

There are emotional changes:

- ❖ You may experience loneliness.
- ❖ You may feel anxious or worried.
- ❖ You may feel abandoned.
- ❖ You may feel guilt and regret because you wonder if you did enough for your loved one.
- ❖ After a prolonged and difficult illness, you may even feel the normal reaction of being relieved.
- ❖ You may feel that nothing matters like it did before.
- ❖ Many people, when they first experience grief, feel shock or numbness.
- ❖ You may be restless and find it hard to sit still.
- ❖ Often those in grief become frightened because they may be faced with a change in companionship, home, job, or financial support.

There are mental changes.

- ❖ People who experience grief often become forgetful and have difficulty concentrating.
- ❖ Some become confused and struggle to complete previously simple tasks.
- ❖ There may be a lack of interest in daily affairs.
- ❖ Questioning the meaning and purpose of life is another possible reaction.

There are other changes:

- ❖ At times a person may expect a loved one to call, or they may be sensing the loved one's presence, seeing her, or hearing his voice.
- ❖ Because of the very personal and tender nature of grieving, a person may want to isolate and withdraw socially.

Why must I grieve? Won't the hurt go away after time passes?

Healing wounds of the heart is different from healing physical wounds. Given time, most physical wounds will heal by themselves because the physical body usually heals over time. Hurt that results from the loss of someone we love can only truly be healed through active grieving.

It is true that we can cover over grief through drugs, alcohol, activities, another relationship, or just by mentally pretending that we feel okay. The problem is the wound still exists inside of us, and will affect our ability to enjoy life fully and to love others.

In our culture, we are not taught the skill of healing the heart, healing emotional wounds. You may discover that it is difficult to find people who are willing to listen to your hurt in a non-judgmental and comforting way.

A simple way to remember what is needed to heal grief is:

"What you can feel, you can heal."

what you may be experiencing as you are grieving

Grief that results from a loss of a loved one is a unique experience that often results in changes that surprise most people. You may find it helpful to understand what you may encounter on your healing journey.

- Your grief may take longer than you think, require more energy than you would have ever imagined, involve many changes, and may be continually evolving.

- Your grief may show itself in all spheres of your life: psychological, social, mental and physical.

- You may grieve for many things, not just the death alone. You may grieve for what you have already lost, and for what you may lose in the future.

- Your grief may include mourning, not only for the actual person who died, but also for all of the hopes, dreams, and unfulfilled expectations you held for that person.

- Your grief may involve a wide variety of feelings and reactions such as depression, sadness, anger, confusion, and guilt.

- The loss may bring up the old issues, feelings and unresolved conflicts from the past.

- You may find it difficult to care for yourself as you once did.

- You may have trouble with remembering and making decisions.

- You may feel like you are going crazy.

- You may find yourself repeatedly thinking about the deceased.

- Your need for companionship may be different; you may find yourself withdrawing or, conversely, becoming more active socially.

- You may begin a search for meaning, and question your spiritual beliefs.

- Others may have unrealistic expectations about your grieving and may respond in an unhelpful way.

- You may experience powerful surges of grief, which occur suddenly with no warning. These may happen on certain dates, such as an anniversary or holiday, or take place somewhere that reminds you of your loved one.

Adapted from "Grieving: How to Go on Living When Someone You Love Dies," by Therese A. Rando, PhD.

tools to help you with grief

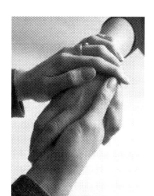

※ Be gentle with yourself. Be patient with yourself.

※ Find supportive, trustworthy friends and share feelings honestly. Feelings are neither right nor wrong; they just are.

※ Allow new people in your life to help.

※ Give yourself time for healing. Allow yourself time to accept your loss, and the time to adjust to the changes in your life.

※ If possible, maintain a "regular" schedule. Maintain realistic goals and expectations.

※ Try to live "one day at a time." Set a goal of getting through another day. Soon those days become weeks.

※ Be aware of your body's need for nutrition and rest. If you notice something worrisome, seek professional help.

※ Honor the messages your body gives you. Unexpressed words or tears can cause lumps in your throat; anger held inside could cause a headache or an upset stomach.

※ Writing letters or drawing pictures about your loss or grief are healing ways to get your feelings out.

※ When the world around you seems to be filled with "land mines" that set off such feelings as anger, loneliness, or resentment, realize that these reactions will pass, and eventually will heal.

※ As a person facing grief, others may not know how to talk to you, and may avoid you. You do not have to make it better for the world. Focus instead on taking care of yourself.

※ Seek support from those who know how to help you heal such as a hospice grief support group or a therapist.

myths about grief

Our culture teaches myths about how we are supposed to grieve. When we believe these myths, we create unrealistic expectations and may criticize ourselves unfairly when they cannot be met. When others tell us that these myths are true, we may find this hurtful and confusing.

As you read the following statements, decide which ones you may need to let go of.

- Everyone grieves in the same way.
- Over time grief declines in a steady fashion.
- It is better to tell bereaved people to "be brave" and "keep a stiff upper lip" because they will not have to experience as much pain.
- It is not important for you to have support of other people in your grief.
- All losses are the same.
- If your grief is "resolved," it never comes up again.
- Losing someone to sudden death is the same as losing someone to anticipated death.
- Being upset and angry means that you do not believe in God or trust your spiritual beliefs.
- Rituals and funerals are not important in helping us deal with life and death.

Myths about Family Grief

- Family members will always help their other grieving relatives.
- You and your family will be the same after the death as before your loved one died.
- There is something wrong with you if you do not always feel close to family members.
- You will not be affected much if your parent dies when you are an adult.

Myths about Grief and Children

- Children need to be protected from grief and death.
- If someone has lost a spouse, she or he will understand what it means to lose a child.
- Children grieve in the same way as adults do.
- Parents always divorce after a child dies.
- Children best heal their grief by talking about it.
- Babies don't grieve.

5

Myths about Grief and Relationships

‣ Once a loved one has died, it is better not to focus on her or him, but to put that person in the past and go on with your life.

‣ You will have no relationship with your loved one after the death.

‣ The intensity and length of your grief are a testimony to your love for the deceased.

‣ If you are a widow or widower, you should grieve like other widows and widowers.

Myths about Personal Feelings When Grieving

‣ Feeling sorry for yourself is a bad thing when you're grieving.

‣ You should not think about your deceased loved one during the holidays because it will make you too sad.

‣ Bereaved individuals only need to express their feelings in order to resolve their grief.

‣ Expressing feelings that are intense is the same thing as losing control.

‣ There is no reason to be angry with your deceased loved one.

‣ If you feel that you are going crazy, you are.

‣ You should only feel sadness that your loved one has died.

‣ You will be better if you put painful things out of your mind.

‣ You have no reason to be angry with those who tried to do their best.

‣ You must be a "sick" person if you have physical problems while you are grieving.

‣ You should feel better because you still have others who are living.

‣ If you are angry with your deceased loved one, it means that you didn't love that person.

Adapted from: "Shattering Eight Myths about Grief" by the Hospice Foundation of America, "Helping Dispel Five Common Myths about Grief" by Alan Wolfelt, PhD

the grieving person's bill of rights

As you do the work of mourning, it may be helpful to be open with others; yet you are not obligated to accept the unhelpful responses that you may receive from some people. You are the one who is grieving and you have certain "rights" that no one can take away from you. The following list is intended both to empower you to heal and to help you decide how others can and cannot help.

1. **You have the right to experience your own grief in your own way.** No one else will grieve in exactly the same way as you. When you turn to others for help, it is best that they do not tell you how you should or should not be feeling.

2. **You have the right to talk about your grief.** Talking about your grief will help you heal. Seek out others who will allow you to talk as much as you want, as often as you want, about your grief.

3. **You have the right to feel a multitude of emotions.** Confusion, disorientation, fear, guilt, and relief are just a few of the emotions you may feel as a part of your grief journey. Others may try to tell you that your feelings are wrong. Find listeners who will accept your feelings without conditions.

4. **You have the right to be tolerant of your physical and emotional limits**. Your feelings of loss will probably leave you feeling fatigued. Respect what your body and mind are telling you. Get daily rest. Eat balanced meals. Don't allow others to push you into doing things you don't feel ready to do.

5. **You have the right to experience "grief attacks."** Sometimes, out of nowhere, a powerful surge of grief may overcome you. This can be frightening, but it is normal and natural. Find someone who understands and will let you talk out your feelings.

6. **You have the right to make use of ritual**. The funeral ritual does more than acknowledge the death of someone loved. It helps provide you with support of caring people. The funeral is a way for you to mourn. If others tell you that rituals are silly or unnecessary, don't listen.

7. **You have the right to embrace your spirituality**. If faith is a part of your life, express it in the ways that seem appropriate to you. Allow yourself to be around people who understand and support your spiritual beliefs. If you feel angry with God, find someone to talk with who won't be critical.

8. **You have the right to search for meaning**. You may find yourself asking, "Why did she or he die? Why this way? Why now?" Some of your questions may have answers, but some may not. Also watch out for the clichéd responses some people might give you. Comments like, "It was God's will" or "Think of what you have to be thankful for" are not helpful, and you do not have to accept them.

9. **You have the right to treasure your memories.** Memories of someone you loved are one of the best legacies that exist after the death. You will always remember. Instead of ignoring your memories, find others with whom you can share them.

10. **You have the right to move slowly toward your grief and heal. Reconciling your grief will not happen quickly.** Try to remember that grief is a process, not an event. Be patient and tolerant with yourself and avoid people who are impatient and intolerant with you. Neither you nor those around you should forget that the death of someone loved changes your life.

Adapted from Alan T. Wolfeld, The Center for Loss, Fort Colin, CO

rituals-a way to heal and honor your loved one

Rituals are something that you do in memory of your loved one, and therefore they are a way to honor her or him. They also may help you develop a healthy acceptance of your loss, and aid you in your healing. Rituals may evoke many emotions. Pay attention to what comes to you as you do rituals that feel appropriate to you.

- Make an altar, light a candle, or send up balloons in honor of your loved one and recall her or him with feelings of gratitude for the journey you shared together.
- Write about your loved one in a journal or address a letter to her or him.

- Share humorous stories about your loved one.

- Pray in a way that is meaningful and honors the deceased.

- Join others in a memorial service for the one who died. This gathering may involve reminiscing about special times and co-creating a scrapbook of important events.

- Choose a memorial tree, bush, or flower, and plant it in a special place where you will visit.

- Let yourself be still as you reflect on your loved one, and accept what you feel.

- Listen to a favorite piece of music that your loved one enjoyed.

- Tell someone about the death of your loved one. Perhaps you could talk about how you've become who you are as a result of having known this person.

- Treat yourself to a massage or bubble bath, which may include using fragrant products.

- Take a trip or visit a place where you and your loved one liked to go.

- Engage in physical exercise to release stress and to relax.

- Reach out and touch another person today—hugs can be especially gratifying.

- Visit the place where the deceased is buried and scatter flower petals over their grave. Set up a memorial space in your home or yard for your loved one.

- Watch movies or videos you made of her or him, or perhaps watch a movie that was one of your loved one's favorites.
- Make a memorial donation to an organization that your loved one would support.
- Go for a walk with another person and share memories.

- Make a scrapbook or fill a memory box with photos, souvenirs, tapes, or cards.
- Make and share an anniversary cake as a celebration of your loved one's life.

- Make a list of how you felt in the first days of your loss, and how you are feeling now.
- Write a poem or draw a picture of how life has changed since you last saw your loved one.

- Make a greeting card with a theme of "It's been a year since we saw each other."

- Make a list of new skills acquired or relationships made during the last year.

feelings of grief before the loss occurs

 You may begin feeling the effects of loss and grief before a death of your loved one actually occurs. These are typical reactions to current and future losses, and are often referred to as "anticipatory grief." Losses can include those associated with caring for someone with an illness, changes in relationships, and the anticipated death of a loved one. Anticipatory grief may actually help you prepare for the losses and decrease the intensity of grief after the death occurs.

Causes of Anticipatory Grief:

Some of the causes of anticipatory grief are related to fears of actual or possible losses:

- Loss of companionship, social life, and change in family roles
- Loss of usual eating, sleep, work, and recreational habits
- Loss of independence
- Loss of control, such as, being able to care for yourself or a loved one
- Fears related to life without your loved one

Signs and Symptoms of Anticipatory Grief:

It is normal to experience these signs and symptoms:

- Tearfulness
- Anger
- Feelings of emotional numbness
- Loneliness
- Forgetfulness
- Feelings of guilt
- Constant changes in emotions or eating habits
- Depression
- Anxiety or feeling fear
- Denial
- Fatigue

What You Can Do:

Here are some suggestions of things you can do:

- Go for short walks when possible.
- Write in a journal.
- Plan for the future.
- Join a grief support group, or seek counseling assistance.
- Make changes as needed but put off major decisions if possible.
- Do the things you enjoy and want to do now. Forget the chores that you can do later.
- Spend time with your loved one, friends, and family or a support group.
- Attend a caregiver support group.

Adapted from: "Grief Counseling and Grief Therapy" by J. William Worden, "Grief Steps: 10 Steps to Regroup, Rebuild, and Renew after Any Life Loss" by Brook Noel, and "Unattended Sorrow" by Stephen Levine.

when it feels like too much...
how you can heal from many losses

Healing from the death of a loved one is difficult. However, there can be circumstances in life when a person is faced with grief from many losses leaving one feeling overwhelmed, thus making healing even more difficult. In addition, if there are additional stressful issues that you are dealing with, these would add to the complexity of your healing. If this applies to you, do not feel you are alone. Surprisingly the need to heal from many losses occurs more often than most people realize. Let's take a look at the circumstances under which a person can be faced with the feeling that "it is just too much."

❖ **the deaths of many loved ones at the same time**

When there is a fatal car accident, airplane accident, or a natural disaster, it is possible that many loved ones can be lost at the same time.

❖ **the deaths of many loved ones within a relatively short period of time**

There can be times in life, possibly within a year or two, when a person is faced with the deaths of many close family members or friends, making it difficult or impossible to heal completely before another loss occurs.

❖ **the death of one person brings up previous unhealed losses**

Because our culture often encourages quickly "forgetting" the loss of a loved one, and "moving on," we do not completely heal. Consequently, the pain of grief is buried within your body, and can be brought to the surface upon the current death of a close friend or family member. It is also possible that watching a movie, looking at a picture, or a number of different ways can awaken delayed grief.

❖ **secondary losses often occur with the death of a loved one**

The death of a spouse, a partner, a parent, a sibling, etc. can leave us with many other losses such as the loss of personal support, finances, living conditions, etc.

If you have experienced any of the above, you may well be feeling that it is just too much to bear, and wondering if you will ever feel at peace again. I assure you that the pain of your grief will diminish, and you can heal.

These are agreements that may be helpful to say to yourself on your healing journey:

❖ "I realize that it will take time to heal, and I will be patient with myself."
❖ "I will ask for support and help when I need it, and not isolate myself from friends and healing activities."
❖ "I will grieve in a way that makes sense to me, and not necessarily what other people tell me makes sense."
❖ "I will take the time to experience my emotions."
❖ "I will care for myself physically."

Guidelines that may help you on your healing journey:

1. **Ask for help.** Healing from many losses is a complex and long-term task; therefore, help from professionals skilled in grief recovery can be extremely beneficial. Your local hospice will have bereavement groups that are available to the public. Also, there are times when it is helpful to seek individual counseling from an experienced grief counselor.

2. **Try to realize that it is helpful to focus on healing from one death at a time.**

It may be beneficial for you to write down in a grief journal the losses that you have experienced, and make a contract with yourself regarding what order you choose to grieve your losses. There is advice given by experienced mountain climbers: "Think only about the next step." Healing from multiple losses is much like climbing a mountain…focus on one loss at time.

3. **When experiencing grief due to secondary losses, ask for support from others.**

When experiencing grief, simple tasks like dealing with finances, shopping, cleaning your home, organizing your life, etc., can be overwhelming. You may be surprised how others would like to help, but don't know how to approach you.

4. **Be actively involved in your healing journey.**

The old saying, "Time heals all," is not true when healing from grief. It is more accurate to say, "Time and effort heals all." You need to be actively involved. You may find helpful suggestions in these articles: "when you are grieving," "the grieving person's bill of rights," "myths about grief," and "tools to help you with your grief."

5. **Try to understand the journey into your grief.**

One of the first steps toward healing is to accept your grief with mercy instead of rejection, and in so doing you can learn to trust your pain enough to explore it. It is the letting go of resistance that opens grief to healing. With multiple losses, one comes to recognize that there is a reservoir of grief that needs to be emptied, one cupful at a time.

6. **Recognize these anchors that will keep you stuck in your grief: guilt, lack of forgiveness, impatience and self-judgment.**

So often, when faced with grief, we become so merciless to ourselves during our healing process through self-judgment and guilt. "If I only could have done something more," "If I only could have been there," or "What did I do to deserve this pain?" If you find yourself anchored by guilt or judgment, try to be gentle with yourself and give yourself credit for all the good things that you did do, and forgive yourself for your limitations.

7. **Try to accept the reality that your life will never be the same again.**

Yes, you will heal, and you will develop deeper understanding and compassion for others, and yourself. The Dalai Lama said, "Without pain there is no compassion." The losses of loved ones bring both gifts and changes that are healthy to accept, and embrace.

after a death by suicide…
struggling to understand

Your loved one has committed suicide. Dying in such a manner leaves friends and families grieving in a much different way than most other forms of grieving. It may be helpful for you to understand these differences so that you are aware of the journey of healing from death by suicide, and the difficulties associated with it.

Unfortunately, many survivors of suicide suffer alone and in silence.

Because of the social stigma surrounding suicide, survivors feel the pain of the loss, yet may not know how, or where, or if, they should express it. As a result of fear and misunderstanding, survivors of suicide deaths are often left feeling abandoned at a time when they desperately need unconditional support and understanding. The feelings of grief are so intense that many survivors wonder if they will ever heal.

The healing journey is difficult, yet you can heal.

There are many things that you can do to begin the process of healing. Here are some suggestions:

❖ **Try to accept the intensity of your grief**. Grief following a suicide is usually complex, and there are many typical reactions of emotional pain. When you least expect it, you may be overwhelmed by feelings of depression, sadness, guilt, fear, anger, and shame. With support and understanding, you can become more accepting of these responses in yourself.

❖ **Work towards the understanding that the suicide is not your fault.** Survivors of suicide often blame themselves for this tragedy and believe they may have caused it, or neglected to do something that could have prevented it. You are not responsible for the suicide.

❖ **Try to accept that you may never understand why the death occurred.** There are many unanswered questions that you will confront, and you may never find adequate answers. Work towards accepting this uncertainty and becoming more peaceful with not knowing "why."

❖ **Don't worry about "losing your mind" and trust that you will survive and heal.** Healing from a loved one's suicide is a difficult journey, and sometimes you may feel you are "going crazy." Realize that you are in a deep grieving process during which such thoughts are typical, but gradually fade.

❖ **Be compassionate with yourself and take care of yourself.** Accept your sadness and self-doubt with kindness as you would for a good friend or close family member. It's important to drink plenty of fluids, eat nourishing meals, and get adequate rest and exercise.

❖ **Seek help from friends, family, and support groups.** You need and deserve the support of others who will listen without judgment, and who show their understanding and compassion. Grief support groups can be especially helpful. They provide a safe place to share your sadness with others who also are in the healing process.

healing from the loss of a spouse or partner

When you lose a partner, you experience a unique, unexplainable pain that seems unending. Just putting one foot in front of the other and getting through each day becomes an overwhelming challenge.

In a room full of people, you feel alone and separate.

Well-meaning friends tell you that they know how you feel, because they've lost a parent, grandparent, or sibling. They don't understand the difference—that you lost your other half, your best friend, maybe the parent of your children, the likely person with whom you planned to spend the rest of your life. You have not only lost your spouse, but also the future that you planned for.

Others may compare your loss to divorces or relationships that have ended, not realizing that they can still see and talk to their former partners. They may continue to share parenting. They may even have hopes of reuniting. For you, none of those things will ever be possible. In addition, you may grieve for your children who will never again have an opportunity to be parented by your partner, unlike children whose parents have separated who can still have a relationship with the other parent.

Healing from the grief of the death of a spouse can last many years.

Although you may at times feel better and go about daily life, you may revisit strong feelings of grief. You may even feel that life is not worth living. In the midst of what may be the most intense emotional experience of your lifetime, you may also face:

- ❖ **Change of identity and social isolation** - You may suddenly feel alone socially because you are not included in the world made up of couples.

- ❖ **Feeling of being disenfranchised** - If you were not legally married, or perhaps a gay couple, people may not give significance to your relationship, and therefore to your loss.

- ❖ **Loss of dreams** - Plans and dreams you made as a couple may no longer fit or be possible.

- ❖ **Financial loss** - With the earning power of one person instead of two, maintaining your former lifestyle may be difficult.

- ❖ **Increased family and household responsibilities** - If you have children at home or work commitments, you may experience pressure to "get on with things."

- ❖ **Increased vulnerability to health problems** - Grieving will leave you tired and exhausted, thus making you more susceptible to illness. (If you have suicidal thoughts or find yourself turning to alcohol or drugs to numb your pain, call a healthcare professional, family member or friend for help.)

Experiencing these dramatic changes in your life may result in:

- ❖ Feelings of sadness, despair, emptiness, anger, depression or guilt
- ❖ Restlessness and sleep problems
- ❖ A sense of inadequacy and concerns about health and well-being

In the midst of these changes, realize that you will heal.
You can put your life back together again.

What can you do to put your life back together? How do you pick up the pieces and go forward? It may not feel like this is possible, but there is hope. Although you can't have your old life back the way it once was, you can build a new one.

You will never forget the partner that you lost, nor would you want to. Moving on doesn't mean leaving your loved one behind or forgetting that the person ever existed. It means moving forward and bringing the memories of your loved one with you, but moving forward just the same.

You can work through your grief.

You can't go over, under, or around grief. Working long hours or keeping constantly busy doesn't prevent the misery - it just delays your healing. The only way to work through the many complex feelings of grief is to experience the pain of your loss.

You may find it easier to allow others to help you heal.

Support groups can be found through churches, hospitals, social service organizations, and funeral homes. If you're not ready to join a support group, *WidowedNet; GriefNet; Grief, Loss and Recovery;* and *ChapterTwo* offer online support and a way to communicate with other individuals who have lost partners via message boards.

Also, your local hospice has support groups that provide a safe place where you can talk about your grief and be listened to with compassion. I have found that people who participate in these groups are often able to heal and to adjust to their new lives more quickly.

Adapted from HealthAtoZ by Diane Griffith

on being alone...suggestions for the widowed

To become widowed is to suffer one of life's most profound losses. When a loving marriage bond is severed, a part of you feels lost. Life will never be the same again. You may be asking, "How can I survive without my spouse?" Yes, you will survive and you can heal and even grow from this sorrowful experience. Perhaps you can find some help from the suggestions of widows and widowers who have preceded you:

❖ **You need time and patience to heal and adjust.**

Whether your spouse's death was anticipated or unexpected, the event of death always seems sudden. In a moment you have become a widow or widower. Your self image may be turned upside down. Your role has changed. The transition from wife to widow, or from husband to widower is a very real, painful and personal experience for which you may have had no preparation. There is much to go through, but with support, healing, and patience you can discover a life for yourself.

❖ **Give yourself permission to mourn**.

To lose your spouse is to lose something of yourself. It is only natural to grieve such a loss. You may suffer emotions that you never thought possible. But even though you are deeply grieving, as difficult as it may be, it is healthy and will help you heal. You made a substantial emotional investment in your marriage, and, whether it was happy or unhappy, those emotions survive long after the funeral is over. At first you may not feel strong emotions. You may be in shock, numbed by your loss. Also, don't be surprised at how little support you are given to truly express your grief. In our culture, most people don't understand the grieving process. Regardless, mourning, expressing your hurt and sorrow, and perhaps anger, is very healthy and healing.

❖ **Learn about the grief journey.**

Most people who have lost a spouse have asked the question, "When will my grief end?" One of the myths about grieving is that it has an ending point, the time when it finally stops hurting. Although grieving continues, most widowed persons find that the intensity and occurrences of their grief lessen. A favorite song, a picture, a special day, etc. can awaken the experience of loss. Grieving is a natural and personal process that has its own pace. It cannot be rushed and it cannot happen without your participation; time does not heal grief without your personal effort.

❖ **Try to maintain your health as best you can.**

The stress of grief weakens your natural immune system. While thinking of staying healthy can be one of the least of your concerns, you might try to maintain your health as best as you're able. Regular exercise, proper nutrition, physical checkups are all a part of maintaining your health. Also, overuse of tranquilizers and other medications, including alcohol, drugs and smoking, contribute to poor health, making it even harder to work through your grief.

❖ **Honor the life you had with your loved one.**

Although your spouse is no longer physically with you, she or he is still present in your heart. Some widows or widowers have created a special place in their home to honor the years that they had together. For example, there can be a place where you put pictures and special mementos, or perhaps plants and flowers in your garden. Or you might consider having a ritual with friends and family for your departed loved one.

❖ **It may be beneficial to ask for help in taking care of the urgent details.**

 Suddenly you are faced with so many urgent details: making funeral or memorial service arrangements, finding important papers, notifying financial institutions, obtaining certified copies of the death certificate, notifying insurance companies and the Social Security office, advising creditors, etc. are all unexpected and overwhelming responsibilities. Consider asking members of your family or special friends to help you in these seemingly insurmountable but important tasks. Asking for help will not only benefit you, but also it will provide meaningful opportunities for others to support you.

❖ **Determine your financial needs.**

Eventually you will be faced with dealing with the day-to-day survival issues. Most people do not like to deal with money management after a sorrowful loss. This can be a frightening prospect. Perhaps consult a tax accountant or tax lawyer who will help you through this process. Try to put off major decisions like quitting your job, selling your house, moving, etc. until about one year has passed. Perhaps taking a leave of absence, or renting your house, or visiting your family, or taking a vacation would be intermediate steps you can take. Possibly family members or close friends can help you determine your income and assets, and weigh them with your needed expenditures.

❖ **It will take time to learn how to live alone.**

With the death of a wife or husband, the way you live, how you perceive yourself, and how others perceive you can change dramatically. It is possible that you feel ungrounded, without direction, and off-center. You may need considerable time to adjust. In a way, living alone may seem like you are starting life all over again. Such an adjustment may well take years. Try to take one day at a time, learn from others who have traveled the same road, and above all, be kind to yourself.

❖ **When the time is right, consider doing things that you have never done before.**

Some widows and widowers find it helpful to reach out to their communities in ways which they have not previously attempted, for example, volunteering in the community, working part-time or returning to school to learn a new skill.

❖ **Consider joining a bereavement support group.**

Bereavement support groups are very beneficial for helping people heal from the death of a loved one. They provide safe places where people who have endured a loss can express their feelings without judgment and find support during their healing journey. Your local hospice will provide grief groups free of charge. If you are comfortable with the Internet, there are many sites where you can go for information and support. A good place to start is *www.AARP.org* offering many helpful and supportive resources suited to widowed individuals and *www.AARP.org/griefandloss* for bereavement help.

Adapted from "On Being Alone: a guide for the newly widowed" by AARP

when your parent has died

No matter how old you are, you are your parent's child. There are still times when you may need your parents. The parent-child relationship often serves as the "mirror" that helps to reflect who you are in this world. Acknowledging the death of your parent can be painful. At first it may be difficult to believe. You can no longer call your parent on the phone, or visit on holidays. The death of a parent may leave you with a broken heart. Perhaps you considered your parent your greatest support, or perhaps there was more you wished for in the relationship. As you search for ways to heal, you may find the following suggestions helpful.

Care for yourself.

When you are grieving the death of your parent, you have special needs. Perhaps the most important need is to have compassion for yourself. Often we do the opposite, and have unrealistic expectations about how to handle our grief "well."

These expectations result from common societal messages that we should be strong in the face of grief. We may be told to "carry on" or "keep our chins up," or "your parent is better off now." In actuality, when we are grieving, we need to slow down, embrace our feelings of loss, and seek and accept support from others.

Good self-care is essential to your survival and to your healing. This doesn't mean that you are feeling sorry for yourself—it means you are allowing yourself to heal. When we nurture ourselves, and allow ourselves the time and attention we need to journey through our grief, we can find new meaning in our on-going lives.

Allowing yourself to mourn.

"Grief" is what we think and feel on the inside when someone we love dies. "Mourning" is the outward expression of our grief, although the words are often used interchangeably. Everyone grieves when someone we love dies, but if we are to heal, we must also mourn. Mourning may include talking to others about our grief, crying, creating a memorial altar, writing in a journal, or participating in a support group. You can honor the significance of the relationship with your parent, savoring what you have learned and will always remember. If your parent died after a prolonged illness, don't be surprised if you feel a sense of relief. This is a normal reaction and there's nothing wrong with these feelings. Also you can take the time to acknowledge and heal any wounds that may still be lingering from "unfinished business."

Tell your story.

A vital part of healing, and an important way to mourn, is "telling your story" again and again. When you tell someone the story of your parent's death, you might relate the circumstances of the death, review the relationship, describe aspects of your parent's personality, and share memories, both good and bad. Part of your story may be about difficulties and conflicts in the relationship that still cause pain. Each time we tell the story, it becomes a little more real. Each time there is another step taken on the healing journey. It's essential to find people who are willing to listen patiently without judging.

17

Be aware of "the big myth."

Some of your friends may tell you, or you may have a voice in your head that says, "Everyone dies, and people who have lived a long, full life are expected to die," or "You are a grown up; you should know about death. You shouldn't be so upset that your parent has died."

The reality is that the death of someone who played such a big part in your life is a profound loss. This is true whether your parent was very old or middle-aged, whether the death was sudden or anticipated, whether you were very close or estranged. Your parent will never be physically present to you again. It's natural to grieve the loss, and to need support for your grief.

Be compassionate with siblings.

Just as there is no single "right" way for you to mourn, there is no single right way for your brothers and sisters to express their grieving.

While you may anticipate some responses, you also may be surprised. Your emotionally detached brother "is a basket case," or your conscientious sister may refuse to help plan the funeral. Try not to let these differences alarm or hurt you. Remember that each one is grieving in his or her own way.

If there is a surviving parent, each sibling will also relate uniquely to that parent. Try to find ways to discuss care-giving responsibilities and vent grievances without blame.

Sorting out physical belongings.

An adult child may find it especially difficult to know what to do with the parent's belongings after death. As with all things in grief, there are no single right answers. It's important to do what feels right. When you are ready to sort through your parent's belongings, ask your siblings or a friend to help you. The task often is too large, and too emotional, to handle alone. Don't dispose of things in haste; you won't be able to get them back later.

Embrace your spirituality as you see it.

Grief is a journey of the spirit that asks you to consider why people live, why people die, and what gives meaning to life. For many, formal places of worship may offer a safe place and a ritualized process to address these spiritual questions. Others may seek solace and answers in reading, meditation, or other contemplative practices. Embracing your spirituality may help to inspire a sense of peace, hope and healing.

Trust your capacity to heal.

If you mourn your parent's death openly and accept support from others, you will, in time, come to reconcile your loss. Ultimately, you may find that you are growing emotionally and spiritually through the grief journey. If you trust your capacity to heal, you can and you will.

Adapted from article by Alan D. Wolfelt, Ph.D., Center for Loss and Life Transition

healing from a sudden or traumatic death...

One of the hardest experiences we may confront in life is the sudden, unexpected death of someone we love. Loss is painful enough, but sudden loss is shocking. The shock multiplies our pain and intensifies our grief.

With a traumatic death, the healing process can be very difficult. People often describe it as feeling like "they are going crazy." Although your experience with traumatic grief and the healing process will be unique, it may be helpful to understand what others have gone through when healing from sudden or traumatic loss.

Traumatic grief generally occurs when a death is:

❖ sudden, unexpected, and/or violent,
❖ caused by the actions of another person, an accident, suicide, homicide, or other catastrophe,
❖ from natural causes when there is no history of illness, like a heart attack or stroke.

There are factors which make this experience even more difficult.

❖ There may be no positive confirmation of the death or no physical body recovered. These circumstances make it difficult to grasp the reality that the death has occurred. Only when that reality is accepted can you begin to move on from the traumatic event to healing the pain that comes from your experience.
❖ Since the death was not anticipated, legal and financial affairs may be complicated. Loss of income can threaten your family's security.
❖ The role your loved one held in the family is lost. It takes time for your family to reorganize and stabilize.
❖ There may be complex organizations, such as the media, legal, and/or criminal justice system involved in your life as a result of the traumatic death.

Common Emotional Reactions:

Shock: Physical and emotional shock may last a long time. Ongoing memories or dreams about the event may occur for months. It may help to break the cycle of recurring thoughts by writing or talking about them.

Fear and Anxiety: You may find yourself anxious or fearful doing simple activities such as being alone in the dark, taking a shower, or opening a closed door. Anxious feelings are a natural, expected response, but when anxiety prevents returning to your usual routines over a long time, it's important to seek help from a physician or therapist.

Guilt: You may experience guilt over things said or done, or not said or done. You may feel guilty for surviving. Knowing that these feelings are not rational does not help to alleviate the pain of guilt and regret. Let yourself find support from a therapist, clergy or a grief support group. Above all, be merciful with yourself.

Denial: Due to the shock of a sudden or traumatic death, it may be difficult for you to immediately accept the reality of the death. This is your body's normal defensive reaction that is designed to help you gradually acknowledge the loss over time.

Anger: Anger and rage may come from the feelings of helplessness and powerlessness you are left with after a traumatic death. Look for a support or advocacy group to help you deal with the anger and sense of victimhood that may result from traumatic loss.

You may feel that your world is shattered.

Sudden loss gives a person no chance to prepare. You may feel "cheated" that you could not say goodbye in the way you would have liked – with special words, a kiss, a hug, or some other act with personal meaning. The loss is one that doesn't make sense, yet you may try to create meaning from the terrible event. You may be searching for answers, and confronting the fact that life is not fair. The world may not feel safe to you. You may become fearful and uncertain, or angry and frustrated. Your beliefs about the world and how it functions may be shattered. You may be questioning your spiritual or religious beliefs. These are natural responses.

In the initial days, weeks, and months, you may go back and forth from numbness to intense emotions.

In general, it may take two or more years for a person to go through the grieving process and adapt to a major loss. With a traumatic death, the time period may be longer. However, the intensity and frequency of painful periods usually diminishes as time passes.

It is possible that you may feel worse a year or more after the death. The numbness that helped protect you in the early months is gone and the full pain of the loss is very real. Your family and friends may have gone back to their own lives, and are not as available to offer support.

Holidays and special family events may trigger intense feelings of grief. When a similar traumatic event occurs, you may feel that you are reliving your experience of loss. Involvement with lawsuits or the justice system can cause upsurges of grief during the entire course of that involvement. If you find coping gets more difficult, it may be helpful to seek counseling.

You may feel out of control because an event has occurred that is beyond your control.

Putting more structure into your daily routine can help you manage these feelings. It's often helpful to keep lists, write notes, or keep a regular schedule. There are new roles to learn, new problems to solve.

You Can Heal.

Although it may be hard to imagine at this moment, try to remember that people do recover from sudden and traumatic loss. You also can ultimately move through this terrible pain and begin to heal. It helps to bear in mind that emotional pain will lessen, and that you will not grieve forever. You can honor your loved one with your memories and ongoing love.

Adapted from "Facing Sudden Loss" by Judy Tatelbaum, MSW, and "Reactions to Sudden or Traumatic Loss" by Barbara J. Paul, Ph.D.

healing when your sister or brother dies

When a sister or brother dies, your world can change in a heartbeat. When such a loss occurs, others may fail to recognize that you, the surviving sibling, face many emotional challenges.

> When your parents die, it is said you lose your past;
> when your spouse dies, you lose your present;
> and when your child dies, you lose your future.
> However, when your sibling dies, you lose a part of your past, your present, *and* your future.

The loss of history

Your family has its own special history and shared bonds. Now that your sibling has died, the bonds are changed, and the family history has a void that cannot be filled. As you grew up together, you and your siblings developed certain characteristics and talents. Some sisters and brothers tend to complement each other by having a balance of interests and skills in different areas. Because you have lost your sibling, you may find your role in the family is changing, and miss the special contributions of your sister or brother in various ways.

The loss of future

After the death of your sibling, special occasions will be different in the future. There will be no more shared birthday celebrations, anniversaries, or holidays with your sister or brother. There will be no telephone calls to announce good news or to seek support. The sharing of life's unique and special events will never again take place with this person, and you may feel the pain of loss deeply each time a holiday or anniversary comes around again. In addition, plans that you made together for helping each other with family concerns such as care of elderly parents or shared property will now be lost.

Siblings can be the "Forgotten Mourners."

Sisters and brothers who have lost a sibling are sometimes referred to as the "forgotten mourners." When a sibling dies, much of the support from family members may be focused on the grieving parents, spouse or partner. The loss of a child, spouse or parent is indeed a very painful experience, which most people recognize. Yet you may experience a lack of understanding for your grief when you have lost a sister or brother. Because you may not receive adequate grief support as the surviving sibling, you may hide your feelings from others, and experience depression, resentment, or alienation.

What siblings may feel:

Guilt and regret: You may have said or done things in a moment of anger that you now regret. Perhaps you were unprepared for the death of your sister or brother, and now wish you had spent more time with her or him. As you became adults, your relationship may have changed from the closeness of childhood. Perhaps your communication became difficult, and you had ambivalence or hostility towards each other. Yet now you may feel guilty because you did not reconcile differences with your sibling and feel regret that there has been a lack of closeness in your family.

Anger: You may feel anger that you have lost one of your best friends. Or you may resent how the family roles have changed with new expectations and obligations placed on you. Perhaps you will now have the primary responsibility to care for aging parents, or you may become the guardian for your sibling's children. Other family members may look to you for guidance and emotional support. These changes may feel overwhelming and add to a sense of anger and resentment after your sibling's death.

Fear of mortality: When a sister or brother dies, it is natural for you to look at your own life. You may question how many years you have left, and how your death will impact the family.

Sadness and grief: When you have lost someone you grew up with, who was perhaps one of your best friends, a void may be created in your life that cannot be filled. You also may struggle with sadness and loneliness as you feel the absence of your beloved sister or brother in so many ways.

Senior citizens who lose a sibling:

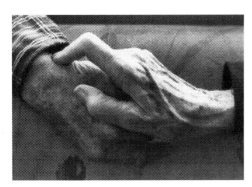

When you are a senior and your sibling dies, your loss can deeply wound your heart. If your spouse and others important to you died before your sister or brother, the grief from the death of your sibling may be more intense. You may be left without the feedback, support, comfort and remembrances you relied on, and feel very alone in your grief. Possibly you will sense from others the belief that there is no need for special acknowledgement or comfort for your loss since it is "normal" for aging people to die. In reality, whether the sibling who died is nine or ninety, the loss can be very painful, and you need compassionate understanding.

Healing from the death of your sibling:

❖ **Continue your connection with your sister or brother.** Even though your sibling has died, a connection still remains in your heart. Surviving sisters or brothers think about, talk about, and remember their sibling at special times such as birthdays, holidays, and the anniversary of her or his death. Possibly the family may create a memorial or have a ceremony on these special days. You do not have to give up your connection to your sibling to move forward with your life.

❖ **Be open to your grief.** It may be that you are putting your grief process on hold as you try to support others in the family such as parents, the spouse of your sibling, or your nieces and nephews. In order to heal, you need to accept your own feelings of sadness and pain. One motto that may be helpful to remember is: "What you can feel, you can heal."

❖ **Look for support in your healing process.** Many siblings find help by talking with others about their brother or sister. Some communities offer sibling support groups, and adult siblings are welcome to attend grief bereavement groups at your local hospice. In addition, you can find support on the Internet: "The Sibling Connection:" *http://www.counselingstlouis.net* offers various links regarding healing from the death of a sibling.

Adapted from "Surviving the Death of a Sibling" by T.J. Wray, "Adults Grieving the Death of a Sibling" and "Death of an Adult Sibling" by The Compassionate Friends, "Loss of an Adult Sibling" and "Experiencing the Death of the Sibling As a Child" by P. Gill White, and "Helping Bereaved Siblings Heal" by Alan D Wolfelt.

healing after an adult child dies

The death of your child, regardless of the cause or age, is painful and overwhelming. You may feel disoriented because a vital part of yourself has been taken away. Perhaps you are thinking, "My child was not supposed to die before me." You, like most parents, expected to die before your child. Your child's death is not something you prepared for, and it seems unfair and untimely.

Your child has always been your child.

Your child, no matter what age, remains your child forever. Even after your child has become an adult, you still have a parent-child relationship. The two of you may have changed your relationship into a more mutual one as adults and perhaps have even become special friends. This doesn't change the fact that you are the one who loved, reared and encouraged your child to develop and grow to maturity.

After the death of your child, you may remember with bittersweet sadness your sense of pride and accomplishment when your adult child completed her or his education, started a career or established a family. It is heart wrenching for you to lose not only your beloved child but also your shared history and dreams.

The complexity and depth of your grief are beyond what words can express.

Perhaps only another parent who has lost an adult child can understand the depth of the pain you may be experiencing. Even if the death was anticipated, you still may feel shocked and numb. If your relationship with your child was strained, or if you did not live near each other for some time, perhaps you now feel regret that you were not closer. If there were unfinished issues between you and your adult child, your pain may be intensified.

If you have grandchildren, there may be additional stress as you become concerned about their care and well-being. It may be that the demands of your own life concerns conflict with the desire to fully grieve the loss of your child. The push-pull of conflicting emotions can be very complex and difficult to cope with. Some of the emotions associated with your loss may be:

- ❖ **A sense of futility:** You may feel a sense of hopelessness because your child's life was cut short. You may even question the purpose of your own life. All of your hopes and dreams may feel shattered. You may be tormented by that unanswerable question, "Why did my child have to die?"

- ❖ **A feeling of guilt:** You may experience guilt for having outlived your child. Perhaps you are questioning if you could have prevented the death. Or you might be thinking, "I wish it was me who died rather than my child." These reactions can be especially intense if your child died as a result of unnatural causes. Perhaps you are left feeling judged, isolated and unsupported.

- ❖ **Feeling abandoned:** If you are elderly, you may have relied on your child for companionship, support, well-being and security. You may be wondering, "How can I make it on my own? I relied on my child for support. I just don't know what to do."

You may find that others discount the depth of your grief.

You may find that other people are not able to comprehend the depth and complexity of your grief. They may feel uncomfortable because they do not know what to say or do. In an attempt to console you, your friends or family may make comments that do not feel supportive or helpful. There is a lack of understanding; therefore you are not comforted by their words. Strong bonds of love and trust were built over the long years of your relationship and the loss of your child is irreplaceable. Know that these thoughts and feelings are a normal part of grieving.

How to survive and heal:

Learning to go on with life and heal after the death of your child is a difficult road to travel and will take time. Here are some suggestions you may want to consider:

❖ **The first step in your grief journey is to allow yourself the time you need to heal.** Remember that healing does not mean forgetting. Accept that your child will always be in your heart. You can honor your child by creating a special place in your home to display photos or mementos. You can also write letters and speak to her or him. Writing a journal may also be helpful.

❖ **You may decide to do something in memory of your daughter or son such as**: establishing a memorial fund, creating a scholarship, making a donation to a charity, giving books to a library or becoming involved with helping others. With these activities, you may feel you can keep the memory of your child vibrant and share the beauty of their life with others. You may be able to pay tribute to your child and find a sense of purpose that is healing for you.

❖ **With your family, consider talking about the death, the loss and the pain.** Revisit the good memories of your child and your life together. Realize that each person within your family will be grieving in their own unique way. It is natural and healing to express feelings and shed tears; however, not everyone is outwardly expressive. Some may use words and some may not.

❖ **Nurture a sense of hope that there is purpose and meaning in your life.** With the passage of time and honoring your grief, painful feelings will lessen.

❖ **Prepare for special days.** Plan ahead for occasions such as anniversary dates, birthdays, holidays and other special times.

❖ **Allow friends to help.** Allowing others to help will give them an opportunity to support you.

❖ **It is often helpful to join a bereavement support group** where you will find a safe and compassionate place to express your feelings, find support, and heal. If you are comfortable with the Internet, you may want to share your grief journey with *www.compassionatefriends.org*, a group that is dedicated to helping parents whose children have died.

Adapted from: "Losing an Adult Child" by Barbara Klich, "When an Adult Child Dies" by Miriam Moss, and "The Death of an Adult Child" by The Compassionate Friends

when your pet has died

You have lost a loyal friend and devoted companion. Your pet has died. It is natural to feel sorrow, express grief and want friends and family to provide understanding and comfort. This help is what you need and deserve.

You have loved your pet, a loyal and devoted member of your family.

You have confided in your animal, who has given you love and support for many years. You may have celebrated your pet's birthdays, and carried pictures in your wallet. So when your pet dies, it's not unusual to feel overwhelmed by the intensity of your sorrow. Your pet provided companionship, acceptance, emotional support, and unconditional love during the time she or he shared with you.

Grieving for your pet that has died may be a more difficult process than grieving for a human.

Sometimes the support given by others, though they are caring, does not feel "big enough" or genuine. Unfortunately, many people think that when your grieving is "just for a pet," it will not be as deep or painful as for the loss of a person. They may even be critical or dismissive of your grief.

When a human loved one has died, friends and family offer support, send cards, flowers, and give food and companionship. This may not be the case when your pet has died. A funeral or memorial service for the deceased person brings people together to provide mutual support and a sense of closure. In most cases, this does not occur with the death of a pet. Hurtful comments such as "Don't be so upset," "It was only a cat," or "You can get another dog," may add to your grief, and to feeling isolated and lonely.

It is okay and healthy to grieve the death of your pet.

- ❖ It is helpful for you to accept that your grief from the loss of your pet is the same as that experienced after the death of a person you loved. Give yourself permission to feel this sadness.

- ❖ Write about your feelings either in a journal, story or a poem.

- ❖ If possible, bury your pet on your property and plant flowers or a tree, and put a picture at the graveside.

- ❖ Create a memorial photo album or scrapbook.

- ❖ Write a letter to your pet.

- ❖ Seek out people who understand your loss. Let others care for you, perhaps by attending a grief support group. There are many pet death chat rooms on the Internet which may be helpful to join. These are some websites:

http://www.pet-loss.net/index.shtml
http://www.petloss.com/

The death of a pet can be traumatic and confusing for a child.

 The loss of a pet may be a child's first experience with death. Children may blame themselves, their parents, or the veterinarian for not saving the pet. A child may feel guilty, depressed and frightened that others she or he loves may be taken away. Here are some suggestions that may help you console a child:

❖ Give the child permission to grieve. Encourage her or him to talk freely about the pet.

❖ Give plenty of hugs and reassurances.

❖ Tell the child's teacher of the pet's death.

❖ Be honest regarding the death of a pet. Say openly, "Your pet has died." Statements like "God took your pet" or "Your pet was put to sleep" may teach your child to fear God, or to become afraid of going to sleep.

❖ Include your child in everything that is going on in regard to the deceased pet.

❖ Openly explain the permanency of death if your child is old enough to understand (refer to the article: "talking to your child about death.")

For some elderly people, their pet is their sole companion.

Many elderly people do not have a strong support system and live alone, away from family. They are at a time in their lives when they are experiencing the deaths of friends their same age. Their pet may become the sole focus of their attention and affection.

For some older people, their pet may have been their last link to the past. The loss of the pet may trigger grief over previous losses. Their pet may have also been a source of security and comforting companionship.

Elderly people may experience more guilt when their pet dies, because they may not have had the finances or transportation to make regular visits to the veterinarian.

Pets also grieve.

Other pets in the household may also grieve the loss of a companion, plus they often sense the owner's sorrow as well. Animals sometimes stop eating, playing or interacting with other household pets when another pet has died. You can help the other pets in the household by keeping their routines as unchanged as possible, going for walks, or playing with toys.

getting through the first anniversary
of your loved one's death

You have gotten through one year of those "awful firsts." For example, your first birthday without your loved one being present, or the first Thanksgiving, Mother's Day, Father's Day, Valentine's Day, your wedding anniversary, or some special day that was unique for both of you. Getting through the first year is hard, and each of these first occasions may bring up the sadness of living without your loved one. After these special days have passed, you may feel that the worst is behind you. But these feelings may continue to arise in future years on special days.

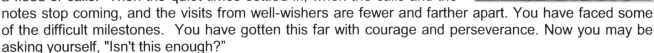

You cannot know what is in store for you during your grief journey. It is different for each of us. After making it through the "year of firsts," you begin to see and know that you will survive. You made it through the funeral or memorial service, read all the condolence notes, and took a flood of calls. Then the quiet times settled in, when the calls and the notes stop coming, and the visits from well-wishers are fewer and farther apart. You have faced some of the difficult milestones. You have gotten this far with courage and perseverance. Now you may be asking yourself, "Isn't this enough?"

Unfortunately, grieving does not "turn off" after one year. Time does not erase the past, but it does provide the space to think about your loved one, heal from the loss, and find meaning. Anniversaries and other reminders, although painful at first, do become easier. These important dates can become opportunities to revisit the happy memories that made your loved one special, and to create memorial traditions.

It may be helpful to be prepared for the first anniversary of your loved one's death.

With the first anniversary of your loved one's death on the horizon, it may be helpful for you to keep in mind that your grief may return with intensity. There are no hard and fast rules regarding grieving, and not everyone will experience intense grief at the anniversary of the death of a loved one. Yet it may be helpful to be prepared for what grief counselors refer to as "anniversary grief." The anniversary of the death of your loved one can be a powerful reminder of your loss. It can be a reminder of all those special days that you had with your loved one. It may also bring up memories of unresolved issues or conflicts.

Before, during, and after the first anniversary of your loved one's death, you and your family and friends may experience a reawakening of the sadness, emptiness, and pain that you experienced when your loved one died. It is not unusual for people to experience behavioral changes for several weeks before and after an anniversary. Withdrawal, angry outbursts, crying spells, overwhelming sadness, lack of attention to detail, loss of interest in school or work activities are fairly common. You may be wondering, "How will I deal with it? If the stress and sadness today is this bad, how horrible will I feel on the actual date?"

You can get through this anniversary, and heal from experiencing it.

Being prepared for the anniversary, and being open to the feelings the event brings, can be a healing opportunity for both you and your family. Here are some suggestions for how to approach the first year anniversary experience:

❖ **Plan for the anniversary.** It may be helpful to know that many people find that the anticipation of the anniversary day can be worse than the actual day. As you anticipate the anniversary, you can bring comfort and healing into this day. Plan what you are going to do ahead of time, even if you plan to be alone, and set yourself up for a "good day." Let your friends and relatives know in advance what your needs are and how they may be able to help.

❖ **You can celebrate the life of your loved one.** The first anniversary of the death is a special day for recognizing your loss. You have not only lost the presence of your loved one, but all of their gifts: the laughter, the love, the shared past and qualities you treasured. Perhaps you are asking yourself how you can celebrate the life of your loved one on the death anniversary. One family took balloons to the high school track where their son had competed, and released them, each with a written personal message. One widow picnicked by the lake where she sprinkled her husband's ashes. Another family had an annual dinner in memory of their daughter.  Creating a positive ritual, either alone or shared with others, can give support, healing and meaning to the death anniversary. (Refer to the article, "rituals, a way to heal and honor your loved one," which suggests further ideas.)

❖ **You can celebrate what you have accomplished together.** The death anniversary is also a day for acknowledging the living. This certainly includes you. The last 12 months have been demanding. You have handled your loss in the best way you could in order to survive. Take time to acknowledge the hard journey you've been on. Then look ahead to the new life you are creating for yourself. Do something special for yourself – perhaps schedule a massage, a special dinner or a trip to a nurturing place.

❖ **Handle your memories with care.** You can choose which parts of the life you shared that you wish to keep, and which parts you want to leave behind. The happiness you experienced with your loved one belongs to you forever. Hold on to those rich memories, and give thanks for the life of the person you've lost. It may be easier to cope with memories you consciously choose to keep, rather than to have them emerge when you are not prepared to cope with them. Perhaps you may decide to create a special place to honor your treasured memories, using photos, mementos and a candle. Journaling your memories will also help you in the healing process.

❖ **Letting go doesn't mean forgetting.** Letting go of what used to be is not being disloyal, and it does not mean you have forgotten your loved one. A part of that person will remain within you always. Letting go means leaving behind the sorrow and pain of grief and choosing to go on. It means you can take with you only those memories and experiences that enhance your ability to grow and expand your capacity for happiness.

❖ **Plan for special support.** It may be helpful to join a support group before and after the death anniversary of your loved one. Your local hospice will have support groups that you are welcome to join. Also, if you are accustomed to the Internet, there are special support groups suited to your exact needs.

You may feel that you will never be finished with grief after the loss of your loved one. Feelings of grief may resurface during many special days for the rest of your life. Each time you will face your sadness on new terms, but may notice that it doesn't seem as intense or difficult. Hopefully, you will be able to affirm how much you have grown and healed in the ongoing journey of your grief.

Adapted from: "The Anniversary Dilemma" by the International Critical Incident Stress Foundation, "A Year Is a Relative Thing" by Ellen Zinner, "What to Expect At the First Anniversary of Loss" by Corinne O'Flynn, "Marking Holidays and Anniversaries" by American Hospice Foundation, and "Anniversary Grief" by Magellan Health Services.

how will I get through the holidays

As you look around during the late Fall through early Winter, there seems to be no escaping the constant messages to be excited, happy, giving, and close to family and friends during the holidays. Yet you may approach this time of year with sadness as you remember loved ones you have lost. There may be a sense of dread about upcoming events and social gatherings. Perhaps you feel pressure to participate when you would rather not. Or you may hope for

opportunities to share special memories but fear bringing them up in order to protect others from feeling the pain of loss. You may want to continue with familiar traditions, but others in your family may want to do something totally different this year.

The expectations may seem overwhelming.

During the holiday season, there are family traditions and rituals that may require more energy than you have to give. You may need time for reflection, or a safe place where you can get support for your feelings of grief and loss. You may be worried about all the things that "need to get done," and at the same time you may be flooded with difficult feelings such as sadness, resentment, guilt, or confusion. If this is the first holiday without your loved one, you may feel lost and overwhelmed, even depressed.

You may struggle with mixed emotions during this time of year. When you are grieving, the pain of missing your loved one and participating in celebrations without her or him may be especially difficult. It is important to be kind to yourself, get plenty of rest, and respect your limitations. Each of us has a personal response to grief and loss, and we each have a different style of coping.

Here are some suggestions to help you cope during times of holiday stress:

❖ Many people who are grieving the loss of a loved one often say that anticipating the upcoming holiday is worse than the actual event itself. It is possible to minimize stress of the holidays by **planning ahead for the activities and tasks you can manage**, and by letting others know what your limits are. Decide what you want to do this holiday season, and don't set expectations too high for yourself and others.

❖ **It may be helpful to recognize the holidays will not be the same this year**. Expecting everything to be the same may lead to disappointment. Decide what each family member can handle comfortably and be careful to avoid "shoulds."

❖ **It's okay for you to experiment with making changes to the ways "things have always been."** Perhaps your family will plan to celebrate at a different time of day with a new meal menu or a different time to open gifts. Or you may decide to hold your family gathering in another setting than the usual one. You may decide to blend new rituals with some of the old ones.

❖ **Take time to reflect on and treasure your memories.** You might write a letter to your loved one, take a walk in a favorite place you shared, or gather photos for an album that celebrates those memories.

❖ **Create a ritual that honors your relationship with your loved one.** This could be lighting a candle, reading a poem you've written, or making a toast at a gathering, and your wish to include her or him. Or you may want to create a special place with photos and objects that acknowledges your loved one.

❖ Although it is often difficult to share grief with children, **it is helpful to be open with children about your feelings.** Instinctively, they know that something has changed. They need to feel safe to express their feelings of sadness, confusion, and disappointment about the holidays being different. This book has articles which may be able to give you ideas about helping your children with grief.

❖ **You may feel you can acknowledge your loss more meaningfully by becoming more involved with your spiritual community, or by doing something for others.** Perhaps you may wish to make a donation in the memory of your loved one, or invite a guest who would otherwise be alone to join your family's gathering.

❖ **Be careful not to isolate yourself.** It may be helpful to take time for yourself and, at the same time, give yourself permission to enjoy relaxing and celebrating with family and friends. Having fun and feeling uplifted does not mean you have forgotten or abandoned your loved one.

❖ Some people fear crying in public, but worrying about crying is an additional burden. **It is usually better not to push away tears. If you let go and cry, you may feel better.** Crying will probably not ruin the day for other family members, and may actually give others permission to freely express their grief in a healthy way. Remember that painful feelings fade and change with time.

❖ **It may be helpful to attend a grief support group** where you can share your feelings with others not invested in what you decide to do or not do during the holidays. Your local hospice may have a public remembrance ceremony for others who have recently lost loved ones.

Celebrate the gifts of your loved one.

During the holidays, you may feel a special emptiness and sadness that you have lost someone close. Whether this person was your father, mother, partner, spouse, child, sibling, or another close to your heart, it may never feel okay that she or he has died. This can feel especially true when there are celebrations of being together and sharing in which you feel the absence of your loved one. Yet you can celebrate this person who is still in your heart and feel gratitude for the gifts you received in the relationship. **Instead of dreading the holidays, you may find that this is a time to acknowledge the love, joy and experiences you shared.** No matter how you do decide to spend the holidays, be gentle and compassionate with yourself and family members. Take time to love and be loved and to continue the healing journey of grief.

Adapted from "Holidays and Remembrances" by Mona Reeva, LCSW, "Getting Through the Holidays for Bereaved Parents" from The Compassionate Friends, Inc. , "Grief during the Holidays" by Hospice Foundation of America, "How to Help Ourselves through the Holidays" by Hospice.net, "Coping with Holidays and Family Celebrations" by Helen Fitzgerald, and "My Friend, I Care: The Grief Experience" by Barbara Karnes

it won't be the same this year…
getting through those special days

"How can I face Mother's Day when mom is no longer living?" "How will I get through Graduation Day when our son, who died so suddenly, should have been among those graduating this year?" "How will I get through her birthday, or our anniversary, or that wedding?" "Every Friday night our family ate pizza and watched a movie; now on Fridays, there's a feeling of emptiness" "I don't know how to get through those special days."

When someone we love dies, we miss them in many ways and on many special days. Thinking of a special day may once have filled you with eager anticipation, but now you may approach it with dread. It is often difficult when that particular day for celebration was a favorite of the person who died. Grief can be very painful on occasions when you got together and shared with your loved one. While friends and family gather, you may feel lonely and sad.

How can I prepare myself to get through those special days?

Here are some suggestions that may help to ease the pain of your loneliness and assist you in your healing process. Please keep in mind that there is no single right way to be with your grief. Do what is most helpful for you. Here are some suggestions:

- ❖ **Acknowledge that it won't be the same this time or this year.** Someone important in your life is gone and you may feel that you are not the same person. Death creates changes we cannot control. Try not to act as if nothing has changed. Your life has changed and accepting this reality can help you begin to move forward. Remember to be kind to yourself during those special days without your loved one.

- ❖ **Many say the anticipation is worse than the day itself.** Prior to upcoming special days, it may be helpful to pay attention to your thoughts. Do you catch yourself with negative thoughts like "I can't handle this." Try to change these thoughts into something more positive, such as "I need to stay focused on the present; I can get through this day."

- ❖ **Express your needs.** Let others know about the special dates so that they can be supportive as you go through difficult times. Let them know what might be helpful and what you want and need for that special day.

- ❖ **Planning ahead for special days can be very helpful.** There are ways to make them meaningful, yet different from the past. The key is to create rituals and activities that honor your personal needs and the memory of your loved one. Perhaps you will choose to do some of the activities you used to do together, while also finding new ways to bring meaning and healing to that day.

Rituals increase the sense of personal power in an otherwise powerless situation.

There is probably nothing that leaves us feeling more powerless than the death of a loved one. When you repeat old rituals or create new ones, you choose symbols and actions that help you to make the transition to new ways of being in your life. Rituals can help you continue the journey of healing,

31

allowing you to express your feelings of grief while helping you to accept the loss of your loved one. Rituals encourage you to remember and honor the relationship that you have lost. They are ways to express the on-going love you feel, even though the person has died.

Some people find comfort in keeping traditions as much the same as possible.

If that is true for you, find ways to remember your loved ones during those occasions when you may miss them the most. Here are some examples of ways to acknowledge and include them:

- ❖ You might want to light a candle at a table to symbolize their continuing presence in your life.
- ❖ Perhaps you would like to write a greeting card and place it where everyone can sign it. You might want to set aside some time to share stories.
- ❖ It can be very comforting to remember your loved one together with family and friends. You might want to choose a particular activity enjoyed by your loved one and do that in her or his memory: singing special carols, playing basketball, eating a favorite dessert, or visiting a special place.

Some people find comfort in creating new and different rituals.

Creating new rituals can be a way to acknowledge and accept that your loved one is gone but not forgotten. It is okay to find ways that honor your loved one without doing old traditions. When you make changes, try to avoid judgmental thoughts like: "I'm being weak," "I'm avoiding reality," or "I'm betraying my loved one." The following are some examples of what other families have done. (Refer to the article "rituals… a way to heal and honor your loved one" for additional ideas.)

- ❖ One family decided to introduce a new tradition - to make a scrapbook of the loved one to display each year as a part of their new holiday tradition.
- ❖ One family decided that instead of staying home after the death of their loved one, they would take a trip together. Just being in an entirely new environment was helpful.
- ❖ Another family made a collage together about their loved one from old magazines.
- ❖ Another family got out a box of old pictures and began looking at them, making comments and sharing stories.
- ❖ One family set a time to give some personal belongings of their loved one to other family members and friends. Consider having a basket ready of personal items to give to others - gifts from your loved one to each person.
- ❖ Some families choose to ignore a special occasion. This does not mean that they have forgotten their loved one. Instead they decided to take care of themselves by reducing the dread of a particular event. When you give yourself permission to discard some things "you have always done before," you may relieve a great deal of pressure.

Whatever you decide, respect your own grief.

When you choose what is meaningful and eliminate what is stressful, you can move toward those special days and, hopefully, find them to be bearable, comforting, and healing. It won't be the same this year. Someone you loved has died. However, your memories will not die. Your rituals and traditions can help you and your family learn how to survive "those days" and how to grow from them.

Adapted from "Getting through Special Days" by Patti Homan, Pathways Center for Grief & Loss; "Those Special Days" by Pat and Russ Wittberger, and "It Won't Be the Same This Year" by Dr. Linda E. Jordan.

a hero's journey...how men heal from their grief

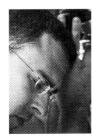 As a man, a grief counselor and a facilitator of a grief group, I would like to talk to you about healing from your grief in a way that I hope will make sense to you, and will work for you. I will state right up front that grief is a problem with no easy solution, especially in our culture where there is a massive denial of death and grief. Regardless of how our culture has influenced you, when you lose someone that you love, someone you depended on and someone who depends on you, it is normal to hurt and feel lost. Your life has changed, perhaps without any warning. It is important to heal from the hurt that you are experiencing. I assure you...you can heal.

Slaying the grief dragon...a hero's journey

When a man experiences grief, he is drawn into an unfamiliar world. The grief becomes the dragon of myth, and he is faced with the decision to go on the hero's journey and face the dragon. By confronting this dragon, he opens himself to an inner quest to heal his grief wounds. He can choose not to fight the dragon, but there is certainly a price to pay. The price is that he will always have the dragon on his heels, breathing fire down his neck. He will find himself unable to engage fully in life. The grief dragon can become a hidden shadow. When that happens, a man can begin to act unconsciously, and can become cranky, bitter, depressed, or resentful, and may blame others for the mood he is in.

On the other hand, when a man is able to courageously face the dragon and not run, when he finds a place to experience the pain, and is able to accept it as a temporary visitor, he has gone on a hero's journey. It takes a courageous man to stand and face the grief dragon. In my experience, a man who has squarely looked at his grief, and healed it, has conquered one of the most difficult challenges that any man can experience, and, through meeting this challenge, will become a more fully functioning and happier person.

How men heal from their grief:

Much has been written about men not expressing feelings. I believe this is because they tend to grieve in a private and quiet manner. Many people believe that the healing of grief is only accomplished through crying and talking about it. While these are two possibilities, there are other ways. It's more useful to focus on the strengths men possess. Men typically value autonomy and action. Although each individual, man or woman, is unique, men may be less efficient at processing feelings verbally. Action can be used by a man as a catalyst for getting in touch with his grief.

A man may tend to be more private in his grieving process, and could be inclined toward *doing something* to connect to his grief. A man's action can serve as a ritual connection to grief when he makes a conscious link between the action and the loss. Each time he performs an action, it activates the grieving process and moves him towards healing. Unfortunately, our culture generally subcontracts male grief actions to funeral homes. We know that in the past tasks such as making a casket, digging a grave or doing other physical things associated with death were part of men's responsibilities. These actions have been assumed by organizations, leaving most men alone in their grief.

Whether a man knows it or not, his own receptive allowing will affect all those around him; rain will fall on parched fields, and tears will turn bitter grief to flowering sorrow, while children dry their eyes and laugh. Knowing Woman by Irene Claremont deCastillejo

Men's healing through activity:

Let's take a look at some examples of action that might help you connect you to your feelings associated with grief. As you "take action," remember to pay attention to the feelings behind the action. This can be a powerful way to heal *if the activity is connected with the pain of grief.*

1. Participating in the funeral or memorial service. At the memorial service consider saying a few words about your loved one, or carry a picture of your loved one in front of the casket, or arrange a collage of pictures of your loved one for the reception.

2. Write a poem, a song, or a letter to your loved one. Try to be aware of your feelings as you write.

3. Make a scrapbook. Put together a picture scrapbook of your loved one and call friends and family together to discuss the pictures and share memories.

4. Visit the grave site. Perhaps bring flowers and speak to your loved one.

5. Express your anger. Men often are able to get in touch with their grief through their anger, really expressing it...loudly, with movement and passion. One man, whose infant son died, took a set of old dishes, went to the city dump, and broke every piece.

6. Create a memorial in honor of your loved one. One man built a pond for his brother who was killed; another planted a flower garden in the shape of a heart for his wife, and another planted a tree over the place where he buried his dog. Also, you can post a memorial on the web: *www.griefworksbc.com/HonourPage.asp*

> *"We love and miss you even though you are gone. You are in our minds and in our hearts. Your love keeps us safe and strong. Can't wait till the day we meet again. No more tears or sad songs. I love you now more than ever. You're the only one in my mind when I sit and cry all alone. We love you dad. Love, your son, Andrew."* Written by a son whose fisherman father was lost at sea off the Northern California Coast. This son created a memorial on the Eureka, California pier.

7. Use something that belongs to your loved one. One son, whose father was killed in an airplane crash, fixed up his dad's old truck and drove it to work.

8. Console others who are grieving. Helping others who are grieving will often help a man get in touch with his own grief.

9. Join a grief chat room on the Internet devoted exclusively to men: *www.webhealing.com/honor.html*

10. Join a support group. This is a safe place to talk about your sorrow. It often helps men get in touch with their feelings by being in the presence of other men and women grieving their loved ones.

Adapted from "Men and Grief," by Susanna Duffy, "Grief and Men," by Carole Staudacher; and "Swallowed by a Snake: the Gift of the Masculine Side of Healing," by Tom Golden.

helping your loved one who is dying

Your loved one, who is someone you care deeply for, is dying. This is an extremely difficult time for you, your loved one, and all who care about her or him. You may be asking yourself, "How can I be of best help and comfort?" Here are some suggestions that may be a useful guide:

You can begin to help your loved one by accepting for yourself the painful reality of her or his impending death. You can allow the gradual process of letting go unfold for each of you, recognizing that your loved one's journey needs to be validated and respected. It may not be until she or he actually dies that you can finally acknowledge the reality of your loss.

Perhaps the greatest gift you give your dying loved one is the gift of your presence.

If it is possible, visit your loved one at the hospital or at home—not just once— but as often as possible. Rent a movie and watch it together. Play cards or games, or perhaps read to her or him. Simply sitting and being present will say to your loved one, "I am willing to walk this difficult road with you and face with you whatever comes." Also, respect your friend's need for alone time; sometimes she or he may not be up for company.

If you are unable to visit your sick friend due to distance or other circumstances, write a letter. Tell your friend how much she or he means to you. Reminisce about some of the fun times you've shared. Do your best to write again soon. If you're not comfortable writing, consider sending a video or audiotape of "notes" to your friend. Or simpler yet, pick up the phone.

Through listening well, you can help your loved one cope during this difficult time.

Your physical presence and desire to listen without judging or giving advice are valuable helping tools. Give your friend permission to express her or his feelings about the illness without fear of criticism. This will help your friend feel heard and understood. Think of yourself as someone who "walks with" not "behind" or "in front of" the dying person.

Avoid saying "I know just how you feel." Comments like, "This is God's will," or "Just be happy. You have had a good life" are not helpful. Instead, they hurt and make your loved one's experience with terminal illness more difficult. Simply letting your friend know you love and accept her or him is support that can help and give comfort.

You will be better able to help your friend if you learn about her or his illness.

If you educate yourself about the illness and its probable course, you will be a more understanding listener when she or he wants to talk. You will also be more prepared for the reality of the last stages of the illness.

Your friend may want to talk about the impending death, or may want to avoid this discussion. The key is to follow your friend's lead. Keep in mind that your friend will experience this illness in her or his own unique way. Allow your friend to talk about the illness at her or his own pace.

Your dying friend may need help with the activities of daily living.

Preparing food, washing clothes, cleaning the house, or driving your friend to and from medical appointments are just a few of the practical ways of showing you care.

Remember to nurture yourself as well as your friend.

Someone you care deeply about is dying and will soon be gone. Find support from others who can listen without judgment as you talk about your own feelings. Take good care of yourself. Eat nutritious meals. Get ample rest. Continue to exercise. Spend time doing things that make you happy.

Helping a dying friend may be very difficult.

 Be compassionate with yourself by accepting your limitations. Not everyone can offer ongoing, supportive friendship to someone who is dying. If you feel you simply can't cope with the situation, try to understand your reluctance and learn from it. Ask yourself, "Why am I so uncomfortable with this?" and "What can I do to become a more open, available friend in this time of need?"

As you go through this process of self-understanding, stay in touch with your friend in the best way that you are able. Perhaps make a phone call rather than a visit. Write a note if you can't bring yourself to phone. Friends and family often abandon people with terminal illnesses, leaving them lonely and depressed. Let your friend know that this situation is difficult for you, and at the same time, acknowledge that your friend's fears and needs come first.

Also, it is important to pay attention to your own energy level so that you do not become exhausted. Trying to do too much may result in you becoming overwhelmed. As a result, you may become emotionally unavailable to your friend because of your own tiredness.

After your friend dies, you will need to mourn the loss.

It is difficult to heal unless you openly express your grief. You may feel confused, overwhelmed, or cut off from yourself and others when your grief is denied. If you embrace your grief and the healing process, you can move on with life.

It may be helpful to remember that grief is a process, not an event.

Be patient and tolerant with yourself. The death of someone you loved changes your life forever. You may want to seek support for yourself.

Adapted from "Helping a Friend Who Is Dying" by Dr. Alan D. Wolfelt

helping your teenager cope with grief

Each year thousands of teenagers experience the death of someone they love. When a parent, sibling, friend or relative dies, teens can feel the overwhelming loss of someone who helped shape her or his developing self-identities.

What Teens Need from You:
Teens need for you to be a caring adult who will let them know that it's all right to be sad. They may also feel other emotions such as anger, confusion and numbness. They need to know that whatever they are experiencing is okay. It's helpful if you share your own thoughts, concerns and feelings and allow them to see you express your grief. Sometimes adults don't want to talk about death and assume that this will spare young people some of the pain and sadness of loss. The reality is that your teen is grieving, and if the subject of the death is ignored, she or he will suffer from feeling isolated and alone.

Rather than waiting for teens to start a conversation, it's **helpful to ask them if they want to talk about the loved one's death.** Be open about your own feelings or difficulties regarding your loved one's death. Then just listen, without judgments or solutions. It's okay to share and discuss your religious beliefs, however, try not to react negatively if your teen is expressing beliefs that are different from the accepted family practice. Older teens are likely to be developing their personal faith practices

and need to feel respected for their individual choices. When you are the adult companion to a bereaved teen, particularly if you are a parental figure, you may become the target for their anger and even cruel remarks. This can be especially difficult to tolerate if you are experiencing your own grief. Try not to respond in ways that will put up walls between the two of you. You may be able to shift the focus when you reflect back to them something like: "It sounds as if you are angry. Could you tell me more about what you are feeling?" Hopefully, the teen will be able to express some of the underlying pain they are trying to mask with hostility or withdrawal.

What You Need to Know about Your Teen's Grief:
People of all ages struggle with the death of a loved one, but adolescents may face especially difficult adjustments following the death. Teens are already going through tumultuous changes in body image, behavior, relationships, and emotions. As they break away from their parents to develop their own identities, conflicts often arise within the family system. A teen typically needs to create some distance from parents or guardians at this stage in their lives, yet this can complicate their experience of grief. For example, if a parent dies during a time when the teenager may be emotionally pushing the parent away, the teen can be left with a sense of guilt and "unfinished business."

At the same time your grieving teen is confronted by the death of someone she or he loved, your teen also faces pressures in their school and social environment. Teens are doing schoolwork, trying to fit in with their peers, perhaps working part-time, or helping with family responsibilities. Even though teens may be physically developed and seem to be as mature as adults, they need your support and compassion.

Many Teens Are Told To "Be Strong."
Many adults who lack understanding of their own grief experience may discourage teens from sharing theirs. Bereaved teens may display signs that they are struggling with complex feelings, yet they may feel pressured to act as though they are doing better than they really are. When a parent dies, a teen might be told to "Be strong," or "Now, you will have to take care of your family." Some teenagers assume they need to be stronger than they are capable of. When an adolescent takes on the responsibility to care for the

family, it may rob them of the opportunity to do healthy grieving. Teens may feel as if they will not survive the pain of their own grief, and be overwhelmed trying to support the rest of the family.

Teens Often Experience Sudden Deaths.
The loss that teens experience often comes suddenly and unexpectedly. A parent may die of a sudden heart attack, a sister or brother may be killed in an auto accident, or a friend may commit suicide. The very nature of these deaths can result in a sense of numbness, trauma, and shock.

Support May Be Lacking.
Don't assume that adolescents have supportive friends and family who will be continually available to them. In reality, this may not be true at all. Sometimes we imagine that teenagers will always find understanding and comfort from their peers. Teens may find that unless their friends have experienced grief themselves, they may ignore or minimize the subject of death in order to avoid feeling helpless.

Signs a Teen May Need Extra Help:

There are many reasons why healthy grieving can be especially challenging for teenagers. Some grieving teens may behave in ways that seem inappropriate or frightening. Be aware of symptoms of chronic depression: sleeping difficulties, extreme isolation, restlessness, signs of low self esteem, talking of suicide, academic failure or indifference to school-related activities. Other behaviors to be aware of might include:

- eating habits may change
- deterioration of relationships with family and friends
- risk-taking behaviors such as drug and alcohol abuse, fighting, and sexual experimentation
- denying emotional pain while at the same time acting "like everything is fine."

To help a teen who is having a particularly hard time with her or his loss, explore the full spectrum of helping services in your community. School counselors, hospice, spiritual communities, and private therapists are appropriate. The important thing is that you help the teen find safe emotional outlets.

Support Groups Are Often Helpful.
Peer support groups are one of the best ways to help grieving teens heal because they're more likely to trust other teens. In a teen grief support group, teens feel safe to tell their stories as much and as often as they like. They may be able to acknowledge that the death has resulted in their life being forever changed. You may be able to help teens find such a group. Also, there are web site-based groups devoted exclusively to teen grief. A list of these can be found in another article: "teens help other teens on the Internet with death and grieving..." Also you can contact the "Dougy Center" for a list of teen support groups in your area: *http://www.dougy.org/*

Understanding the Importance of the Loss:
Remember that the death of someone loved is a shattering experience for an adolescent. As a result, the teen's life is under reconstruction. Consider the significance of the loss and be gentle in all of your helping efforts. Grief is complex. It will vary from teen to teen. Caring adults can communicate to teens that they don't need to hide or be ashamed of their feelings. Let them know that grief is a natural expression of love for the person who died. With love and understanding, adults can support teens through this vulnerable time and help make the grief experience a valuable part of a teen's personal growth and development.

Adapted from "Helping Teenagers Cope with Grief" by Alan D. Wolfelt, "Guidelines for Helping Grieving Teens" by Tom McLeod, and "The Grieving Teen" by Helen Fitzgerald.

teens help other teens on the Internet
with death and grieving

if you are teen, you may find it very helpful to talk with other teens about topics that concern you, including death and grieving. There are several free, quality online sites where you can speak openly and anonymously with other teens and professionals in order to get support and information. Another option might be to join a grief support group for teenagers. Below you will find one online conversation that took place between a teen and staff member.

"Take time to cry and heal."

"I just need to talk to someone. In 9 days it will be the anniversary of my father's death four years ago. I never took it too well and refused to talk about anything dealing with my father. I didn't even cry at his funeral. Since then I have screwed up my life so bad. Can someone help me? But I guess that's not really the big problem. I just feel so fake. I don't want to die, but I don't want to be here. I am tired of smiling and acting happy when really I am so unhappy. Just tell me, what is wrong with me?" Mary, 17 years.

"Hi, Mary. You are obviously still extremely emotional over your father's death, which is completely normal. There is nothing wrong with feeling confused and scared. It is so hard to lose a person who is such a big part of your life. I think that because the anniversary of your father's death is coming closer, you are starting to think about what has happened with your life and what you should do about it. This is good in a way, because by asking for help you are trying to put the past behind you and move on.

Some people tend to hide away their emotions when something painful happens to them, because they think if they don't cry, they won't feel the pain. Unfortunately this isn't true. Sometimes you need to cry to get through things, because otherwise your emotions continue to build up inside of you until one day they will be too much to cope with. Mary, you have got to let them out. Go ahead and cry for your father. No one will think any less of you and it would do you a world of good.

Once you stop trying to hide your feelings away, you won't feel so 'fake' as you called it. You will feel much, much better and it will help you to move on and start enjoying your life without feeling worthless. Life is too precious to waste, and I'm sure that your father wants you to be happy, and for you to find ways to heal. I am always here if you need to talk. Good luck and keep smiling." Judy

www.teencentral.com An anonymous web helpline developed by experts in teen counseling and psychology. It is professionally monitored, password-protected, for teens and by teens, sponsored by KidsPeace, a leader in teen crisis counseling.

http://groups.teenhelp.org/index.php Free online help for teens offering e-mail support, articles, and chat rooms. At this site there is a special link for "teen help with death and grieving."

www.teenadviceonline.org A free forum for teenagers on various topics concerning teens.

http://www.thehealingplaceinfo.org/index.html The Healing Place offers grief support for children and teens dealing with grief associated with the death and loss of loved ones.

http://www.thedougycenter.org has a list of teen support groups in your area.

talking to your child about death

There has been a death in your family, and you see a deep sadness in your child. When you see your child grieve like this, you wonder how you can best comfort and support her or him.

Today children have to be told about death.

In the past, when people were born and died at home, death was a natural part of everyday life and children took part in that event with everybody else. Also more people lived on farms and witnessed the birth and death of animals. This helped children understand the cycle of life.

If possible, teach your child about death before the death takes place.

An understanding of what death means does not enter a child's picture of the world by itself. In most families, parents don't think about explaining death to their children until a person or a pet dies. Children can be taught that death is a part of life when parents prepare them for an expected death in the family.

Sorrow and death are much easier for a child to deal with when they know something about it beforehand.

By making preparation a part of everyday life, the reality of death can be a natural thing for a child. Flowers that wither and die, or an animal that dies, may provide an opening for a discussion. It is possible to talk about elderly people whom the child knows while you talk about yourselves getting old and dying. To help the talk, your local library can provide a list of children's books on the subject.

Talking to your child after a death takes place:

When a family member dies, children react differently than adults. Preschool children usually see death as temporary and reversible. Children between five and nine begin to think more like adults about death, yet they may still believe that it will never happen to them or anyone they know. During the weeks that follow the death, it is normal for some children to continue believing that the family member is still alive.

Children do not need protection from death. Be honest about death and about sorrow.

When your child is protected against sorrow, they will still react when they realize what has happened. No one can avoid grief; we can only postpone it. Trying to protect a child by not telling them of the death may cause them unnecessary anxiety and perhaps even guilt.

Once your child has accepted the death, she or he may display feelings of sadness often and over a long period of time, and at unexpected moments. It is recommended that the family spend as much time as possible with the child, reassuring the child that she or he has permission to show feelings openly and freely. Young children tend to "talk" about their grief through the medium of play.

Anger is a natural reaction for some children when the person who has died was essential to their sense of security. The anger may be revealed in boisterous play, nightmares, irritability, or a variety of other behaviors. Often the child will show anger towards family members.

Children need competent guidance and satisfactory answers to their questions.

Listen carefully when a child asks a question. Make sure you understand what they want to know.

Answer their questions. If your child asks "Am I going to die?" explain that they will, but not for a long time. If a child asks whether a parent is going to die, they should be told that all people die eventually, but that their parent will not die for a long time.

Children ask questions in a very direct way. They may not talk about feelings as much as about more concrete circumstances.

Perhaps they will ask what a coffin looks like on the inside, whether lying in the ground is scary and lonely, or whether it is cold and dark down there. It is important to be prepared for these questions. When the child notices that a parent is uncomfortable, they may stop asking questions. A child will watch to see whether they are allowed these kinds of questions and what reactions are created.

Bear in mind that children do not sit down and discuss a subject for hours on end. They may suddenly ask you some of the hardest questions in the world and give you little time to think answers through. After a couple of minutes, they might want to go back to their playing. Seizing the moment is important. Talk about the subject when they want to. It is natural for them to change the subject and then return to it later.

When telling a child that someone has died, make sure the word "died" is used. Children do not understand indirect statements. Some children have waited years for a grandparent to return because they had been told she or he had "'passed away." These roundabout ways of describing death may help an adult feel better, but they won't help a child understand what has happened. Also, statements like "God took your friend to heaven" are not helpful.

When you are mourning, let your child know it.

It's okay to let your child see that you are truly sad. If grief is hidden, the child will think that grief is not an acceptable feeling. A child may ask a question that a parent cannot answer. It is also okay to be honest and reply, "I don't know."

When children go to funerals:

A funeral is a ceremony that helps people accept death. The child is a part of the family and it is natural for them to take part in the funeral along with everyone else. Prepare them for what might happen at the funeral. Tell them exactly what is going to take place and why. Tell them that some people attending may be upset, withdrawn, or crying, and these are normal reactions.

If a parent's own grief prevents them from talking to the child to prepare them for the funeral, another close relative or friend can do it.

Whether or not to take part in the funeral should be the child's choice. If they don't want to go, ask them why not and let them talk about their feelings. It is not helpful to try to force a child to go.

Helping a child to remember:

It is always good for us to remember our loved ones who have died. Through memories, the person is kept alive in our minds. It is helpful to leave a photo album out for the child to look at pictures of the loved one whenever they like. You can help children hold on to happy memories by asking, "Do you remember...?" or noting "That was how he wanted it" or "This was her favorite food." A child will know that it is good to remember.

Adapted from a text by Christel Bech, RN, *Facts for Families* from the American Academy of Child and Adolescent Psychiatry, and Healing the Bereaved Child: Grief Gardening, growth through grief and other touchdowns for caregivers," by Alan D. Wolfelt.

healing when your child dies-a lifetime journey

A 98-year-old mother was asked, "Where would you like to be buried after you die?" She responded, "With my baby son, Johnny." Sixty-eight years previously, Johnny died shortly after birth, and his mother wanted to be reunited with her son, even in the grave. This mother was my mother, and her request symbolizes the eternal feelings of loss and of connection parents have with a child who predeceases them. Healing from the loss of a child is a parent's lifetime journey.   Bob Dorsett

"Why do I grieve so deeply?"

No one can truly answer this question except a parent who has lost a child. The breaking of this earthly bond prematurely leaves parents grieving not only the death of their child, but also for their own feeling of loss of self…parents whose child has died often say that a part of them has died.

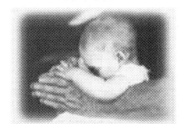

> There is a land of the living
> And a land of the dead
> And the bridge is love.
>
> Thornton Wilder

"Can I survive the shipwreck of my hopes and my dreams?"

Your grief is great, and yet I shared this very simple and true message: "Your life is forever changed yet you can survive this ordeal, and heal. The journey is long and difficult; however, if you understand the healing process, and are willing to do the work by taking small steps, your heart naturally wants to heal, and will heal."

"I feel as if I am going crazy! Am I?"

What you are feeling is normal. This is a time in life when intense reactions, which are usually thought of as being abnormal, are perfectly normal:

- ❖ You may feel stunned as though you are in a dreadful dream. Life may not seem real.
- ❖ You can't believe that your child has died, and you may fantasize that your child is alive.
- ❖ You may search for something you could have done to prevent your child's death.
- ❖ Your body may protest the death in a physical way through sighing, weeping, or no tears at all, exhaustion, shivering, inability to eat or sleep, or have symptoms similar to your child.
- ❖ You may experience outbursts of anger at God, yourself, the doctor, or even at parents who have healthy children.
- ❖ You may have feelings of despair and depression, hopelessness and helplessness. Your inner world may seem flat and colorless, and a dull ache of sorrow may inhabit your being.
- ❖ Like the waves of the ocean, your emotional life and your tears alternate between quiet seas and turbulent waves.

"How can my family cope?"

Siblings: After the death of a child, siblings are at times referred to as "the forgotten mourners," and their grief is often misunderstood because children grieve differently than adults. In addition, depending on the age of the child, their understanding of death may be different than that of an adult. It may be helpful to

read the article in this book, "talking to your child about death," and "helping your teenager cope with grief." Siblings could feel guilt because they survived their sister or brother who died, or perhaps because they said something negative to their sibling before the death. Because you may be preoccupied with your own grief, your child could feel abandoned. The most important thing to remember is your living children do need help and yet you may feel exhausted and not available. Consider reaching out to others for support. For example, there are groups for children who are grieving. Perhaps check with your local hospice, or "The Dougy Center," which has a list of available children's groups and counseling services: *http://www.dougy.org.* Also "The Healing Center, a place for loss and change" has information to offer: *http://www.thehealingplaceinfo.org/index.html*

 **Your Spouse:** The death of a child may put strain on your relationship. Often this is the result of different styles of grieving. One person may express their grief outwardly and another may be private about their sorrow. Grief may have an isolating effect…some people prefer to be alone in their grief, and may not be available as they once were. Try to remember that different styles of grieving are perfectly normal. The Compassionate Friends is an organization dedicated to helping parents whose children have died, and they may have a local chapter for you to contact: *http://www.compassionatefriends.org/home.aspx.*

Grandparents: Grandparents are often referred to as "the forgotten mourners," yet they grieve not only for the loss of their grandchild, but also for the grief that their child is experiencing. Very often grandparents have the same intense grief reactions that their children have.

"What can I do to heal?"

- ❖ Try to be patient during the healing process, and to recognize that it will be gradual, and there is no specific timeline. Healing is a lifelong process.
- ❖ Also try to admit to yourself and others that your grief will at times be overwhelming, unpredictable, and exhausting, and should be expressed.
- ❖ Look for those people who can listen to you without judgment, and with understanding. Consider grief groups with parents of deceased children.

- ❖ Choose ways to express your feelings that best suit your needs. Some suggestions might be: journaling, art, poetry, or any creative activities.
- ❖ If you have a particular spiritual path, it may be helpful to ask for support from your group.
- ❖ When you are asked, "How many children do you have?" include your deceased child, who is still your child and whose life had, and has significance, no matter how short.

- ❖ Acknowledge the need to desire to talk about your deceased child as well as the events that will be missed and also those that have never been experienced.
- ❖ Commemorate your child's life through rituals. (See the article: "rituals that heal.")
- ❖ Maintain a healthy lifestyle that will include emotional support, healthy foods and exercise.
- ❖ If it is appropriate, volunteer for organizations that in some way help children.

Comforting parents whose child has died: Try to recognize the complexities and let go of any preconceived ideas. The death is overwhelming and may seem overly intense, contradictory, or even puzzling. Listening to the parent's story over and over again, and without judgment, is very supportive. Also, helping parents with chores can be extremely helpful.

Consider These Helpful Reference Materials: "beyond tears, living after losing a child" by Ellen Mitchell; "When the Bough Breaks Forever… after the death of a son or daughter" by Judith R. Bernstein, Ph.D.; "when your child dies: finding the meaning in mourning," by Nancy Stevenson and Cary Straffton; "The Death of a Child-The Grief of the Parents" found on the Internet: *http://www.athealth.com/consumer/disorders/parentalgrief.html*

websites
that will help you heal and find support

General Grief Resources
www.growthhouse.org
www.griefnet.org
www.goodgrief.org
www.webhealing.com
www.lossandrenewal.com
www.beyondindigo.com

Death of a Spouse
www.widownet.org
www.aarp.org/griefandloss
www.seattlewidowed.com

Death of a Child
www.compassionatefriends.org
www.bereavedparentsusa.org
www.dougy.org
www.gerardshouse.org

Death of a Pet
www.pet-loss.net/index.shtml
www.petloss.com

Grief Books and Resources
www.centeringcorp.com
www.compassionbooks.com
www.amazon.com

Inspirational
www.wisdompeople.org
www.journeyofhearts.org
www.dying.about.com

How to Support Someone Who Is Grieving
(...even if you are grieving)

As a hospice grief counselor, I would like to share with you some thoughts regarding how you can support someone whose loved one has died. Lack of information regarding how to care for a grieving person is common in our culture. Many people prefer to avoid talking about grief; however, you may be surprised to know that offering effective support to your grieving friend is much easier than you might think. These are some very simple guidelines:

Recognize and respect your own limits. Everyone has differing levels of availability in helping a grieving person. Knowing and respecting your limits is especially helpful if you are grieving over your own losses. Recognize your limits and don't go beyond them. Be gentle with yourself. You may be able to only make a phone call, or send a condolence card. If you don't feel up to it, forcing yourself to make a personal visit may not help your grieving friend. She or he may sense that you are not totally present, and your visit may not result in the support you hoped for. It's okay to explain to your friend that you are grieving and therefore not as available as you would like to be.

Understand the grieving process. A grieving person will often experience many intense and frightening experiences including despair, anger, guilt, and fear. He may be very forgetful, and become easily exhausted doing the simplest tasks. She may cry for hours, or withdraw. Some may yell at God. For no apparent reason, she may appear just fine, only to be revisited by unpredictable highs and lows. "Grief attacks" may come suddenly, without warning, in the most unexpected places. Healing from grief has no timetable; it could take many months, or even years. Be sensitive to the reality that your friend may never fully "get over" the death. The pain may lessen, but sadness may never completely go away.

Cultural sensitivities in grieving. If you sense that there may be cultural customs when you are offering support, it is best to ask the grieving person what support feels most comfortable.

The bereaved need to know that what she or he is experiencing is normal. Many grieving people think they are going crazy. They need to be reassured that what they are experiencing is normal and will eventually pass. With time and support they will heal. Life may not ever be the same as before the death, however, the difficulty of the healing process will eventually subside.

Your gentle, non-judgmental, accepting presence is what your friend needs. Remember that your grieving friend's heart wants to heal, and will heal. You are not the healer but your compassionate presence will offer support as your friend does healing work. There's nothing that you really need "to do" other than being present in an accepting and caring way.

What you can say to someone who's loved one has died:

- ❖ "I wish I had the right words, just know I care."
- ❖ Use the word "died" rather than phrases like "passed on" or "gone to heaven." Your candid words tell say that you are open to her reality.
- ❖ "You and your loved one will be in my thoughts and prayers."
- ❖ If your friend apologizes for crying, you can assure him that it is perfectly normal, and that you are there to support him. Share that you would like to hear how he feels.
- ❖ Don't be afraid to say words that trigger crying. Crying helps healing. Some examples might be: "What do you miss about your husband?" or "Would you feel comfortable telling me about how the funeral was for you?" To heal, it helps to feel.

- Ask your friend, "What I can do for you? I'd love to help." Examples might be shopping or running errands, picking up a rental movie, helping with funeral arrangements, helping with bills, doing housework, helping with the children, looking after a pet, taking your friend to lunch, etc.
- Be honest in your communication, and certainly don't hide your feelings. If you don't know what to say, perhaps tell your friend: "I'm not sure what to say, but I want you to know that I care."
- Try to be comfortable by sitting with your friend in silence, without saying anything. Holding her hand or giving a hug will communicate your caring presence.

What you should not say:

Knowing what not to say can be as important, or possibly more important, than knowing what to say. Speaking unskillful words can limit your effectiveness in your friend's healing process. Here are some suggestions on what not to say:

- "Look at what you have to be thankful for. Be strong."
- "I know how you feel." Rather say, "If you are open to sharing, I'd like to hear how you feel."
- "He's in a better place now," "God wanted her to be with Him," or "It was her time to go."
- "There's a reason for everything. You just have to have faith."
- "It's time to get on with your life, and let go." Your friend will know when the time is right.
- "Perhaps you should…." It is usually better to trust that your friend knows what is best for her.
- "My mother died also." Telling your own story, even if similar, shifts the focus from your friend.
- "There's a good grief book you can read." This changes the dialog away from feelings.
- "You told me that story last week." Repetition of the same story helps a person to heal.

 **Be there for the long haul.** Most people will support a grieving person at the time of the death by attending a memorial service and a reception afterwards. After these events, the reality of the death sets in and many grieving people feel very much alone and abandoned. Be there for the long haul by checking in periodically, or by sending a card. Because most people are very uncomfortable around a grieving person, your friend may actually learn to hide emotions. Don't be fooled by the words, "I'm okay."

When children grieve. The younger the children, the less that they will grieve like adults. Understanding grieving children is a unique field of expertise so it may be helpful to seek help from professionals who support grieving children. However here are some simple suggestions:

- Be honest with your child regarding your own grief. Hiding your sadness teaches a child to do so. Don't tell a child to stop crying. Include children in the grieving process but don't make them your confidant.
- Be open to talking about the death experience.
- Don't force children to go to a funeral if they don't want to, but allow them to attend if they wish.
- Help children to find ways to memorialize the deceased person, perhaps by planting a flower, lighting a candle, or making a memorial altar in the house.
- Keep the child's daily routine as normal as possible.
- Realize that children often display their grief through play.
- Children may express their sadness in brief spurts, and at unexpected times.
- Don't give confusing messages like: "God took grandma to be with Him," or "Grandpa is sleeping now."
- Seek help from professionals who understand how children grieve.

INDEX OF ARTICLES